Pastor
on
Track

Pastor on Track

Reclaiming Our True Role

EMANUEL CLEAVER III

Abingdon Press
Nashville

PASTOR ON TRACK:
RECLAIMING OUR TRUE ROLE
Copyright © 2014 by Abingdon Press

This book is printed on acid-free paper.

Library of Congress Cataloging-in-Publication Data

Cleaver, Emanuel, III.
    Pastor on track : reclaiming our true role / Emanuel Cleaver III.
       pages   cm
    Includes bibliographical references.
    ISBN: 978-1-4267-7253-5 (binding: soft back; adhesive : alk. paper)   1. Pastoral
theology.   2. Pastoral theology—United Methodist Church (U.S.)   I. Title.
    BV4011.3.C54 2014
    253—dc23

                                                                        2013048245

14 15 16 17 18 19 20 21 22 23—10 9 8 7 6 5 4 3 2 1
MANUFACTURED IN THE UNITED STATES OF AMERICA

Contents

Foreword

Like Emanuel Cleaver III, Peter Cartwright was a Midwestern pastor who had definite ideas about the role of the pastor. Unlike Cleaver, Cartwright was suspicious of educated clergy, unless they were of "the right stamp and of the right spirit."[1]

What does it mean to be a pastor of the "right stamp" and the "right spirit" for the twenty-first century? What are those characteristics always present? What are the practices never neglected? What kind of ministry will identify with its biblical and historical roots and, at the same time, meet the needs of people? How can pastoral leaders bring hope to congregations wondering if God has a future for them?

Cleaver has definite ideas about the right stamp and the right spirit for today's effective pastoral leaders. He lays out a clear philosophy of pastoral ministry built around five essentials:

1. Vision
2. Leadership development
3. Leading the people
4. Teaching and preaching
5. Discerning God's will

Not only do these essentials relate to one another; they also feed off of each other. While God's vision is the beginning and center for everything that follows, there is no vision without discerning God's will. Leaders are developed around the vision, while teaching and preaching support and advance the vision. But God's vision is not static. There are new horizons and new visions that emerge while doing God's will.

The church and the world cry out for strong and effective pastoral leaders. No one needs or wants autocratic leadership, but pastors need to remember that they are leaders, and the first task of leaders is to lead. People of the church not only want, they expect, strong and compelling, as well as open and collegial, leadership from the pastor. This is a great moment for passionate and compelling pastoral leadership.

A few years ago, Emanuel Cleaver III did what few pastors can do successfully. He followed a pastor with more than a thirty-year tenure. The pastor he followed had led the church to grow from a few dozen people to a few thousand. His predecessor had during those years served on the city council and as mayor of Kansas City, Missouri. And while still the pastor of this congregation, he was elected to a seat in the House of Representatives.

Yes, Emanuel Cleaver III was asked to follow a civil rights and political icon who was also the beloved pastor of St. James United Methodist Church, the only pastor most church members had ever known. And the pastor he followed was his father. Emanuel III made this challenging transition well because of many of the practices he writes about in this book. He was fortunate to grow up with a powerful mentor in his father and surrounded by some of the giants of church leadership. But he also honed these ideas in many years of serving in disparate churches and contexts in which he encountered the struggles of other clergy in discerning what God was calling them to be and do as pastoral leaders.

Some will resonate with the description of pastoral leadership Cleaver describes. Others will be challenged by it. All will learn and grow from this valuable book.

Lovett H. Weems Jr.
Distinguished Professor of Church Leadership
Director, Lewis Center for Church Leadership
Wesley Theological Seminary
Washington, DC

Preface

I grew up in a predominantly African American church in the United Methodist tradition where my father served as pastor (St. James). I was educated in Catholic schools where I participated in Mass every week. In my home church I was raised with the understanding of a pastor as teacher/preacher and visionary. It is from my father that I learned that preaching is the primary tool of a pastor to feed the people and lay out where the congregation is going. My father was constantly sharing the following statement with St. James: "This is what God is calling us to do." This in my mind meant he must have heard from God and discerned God's will. St. James was a church always on the move because the vision was clear, and we always knew as a church what was next in the life of the congregation. I entered the ministry believing that casting a vision and teaching/preaching were critical for the health of a congregation.

It was in Catholic Mass that I saw the priest presiding over the sacraments as a means of leading God's people. The priest in my eyes served as God's presence among the people. It was clear to me that the priest was the leader because he was the one offering the people the body and blood of Christ.

These two perspectives formed my early understanding of what a pastor ought to be. I began ministry believing in the importance teaching/preaching, casting a vision, and leading by way of the sacraments. Over the years my understanding of the role of the pastor has expanded to include developing leaders and staff. Without properly developing leaders, it is impossible to carry out the vision. Lastly, I have come to believe that one cannot pastor effectively without first hearing from the Lord. What this book does is present what I have learned as it relates to what it means to be a pastor: casting a vision, developing staff and leaders around the vision, leading the people, teaching and preaching, and discerning God's will.

Acknowledgments

I want to thank my wife Sharon along with our three wonderful children, Emanuel IV, Isaac, and Alayna, for their patience, love, and inspiration. Sharon has allowed me to travel the globe to learn, teach, preach, and serve for the sake of the gospel. It is because of her that I am able to share with the world *Pastor on Track*. I would also like to honor my parents Emanuel II and Dianne Cleaver for instilling within me the importance of faith and learning. Thank you to my mother for always supporting me. Furthermore, I owe a great deal to my extended family: my aunts, uncles, cousins, siblings, and most notably my maternal and paternal grandparents. They have supported me throughout my life.

Additionally, I want to acknowledge all of the churches I have served over the last eighteen years. I have come to this point in my understanding of a pastor because of all that I learned at Centenary UMC and Epworth UMC, both in Columbus, Ohio, as well as Longview, St. Andrew, Centennial, and St. James United Methodist Churches in Kansas City, Missouri. Who I am as a pastoral theologian I owe to these unique and faithful congregations filled with God-fearing men and women.

Chapter 1
What Is a Pastor?

He gave some apostles, some prophets, some evangelists, and some pastors and teachers.

—*Ephesians 4:11*

It was early on in my ministry and the congregation I was serving was having a big potluck dinner after worship. This was a big deal in the life of this particular congregation. I had given the benediction and began talking with members as I made my way to the fellowship hall for the meal. I made it only halfway before a distraught member came to me in tears to explain a crisis in her life. She and I stepped into my study to talk about the matter further. Meanwhile, all of the members were in the fellowship hall waiting for the pastor to give the blessing so they could eat. Someone even knocked on my door to inform me that everyone was waiting. I told him to have someone else bless the food because it would be a while before I could join the rest of the congregation. I finished consoling the distraught parishioner, and we had a word of prayer. I took off my robe and went downstairs, ready to eat. I expected to find everyone laughing, eating, and having a good time. Instead, to my utter surprise, I found everyone sitting there in silence, not eating because they were waiting for the pastor to say the prayer. I quickly gave the prayer and encouraged everyone to go ahead and eat. As the members were rushing to get their food, I asked an elderly gentleman who passed by why no one else prayed.

1

He replied that they just didn't feel right giving the prayer for the potluck because that was reserved for the pastor.

Those parishioners knew what a pastor was supposed to do. For them it was crystal clear, and they acted upon their understanding each week. The problem was that their perception was a little different from mine. In any other organization this would have been a huge crisis. Imagine a Fortune 500 company where the CEO has one understanding of what his or her job is, the board of directors has another, and the employees have their own concept. It is highly unlikely that the company could effectively achieve its goals. In fact, there wouldn't be any clear goals because everyone would be operating on a different understanding of the role of the leader. People would be functioning on assumptions and expectations that didn't really exist. If there truly were a company like that, the CEO would quickly be fired. The company would surely lose money, and it would be hard to retain employees because of a lack of clarity.

Some might argue that local churches operate like that fictitious Fortune 500 company. Denominational leaders or the church board members believe a pastor ought to operate one way, the pastor has his or her own understanding of the role, and the congregation has a completely different set of expectations. Because no one is on the same page, the church suffers. It may not lose money, but it will lose members, influence, focus, purpose, and relevancy. An organization without a clear understanding of itself and the role of its leader is off track.

Denominational leaders or the church board members believe a pastor ought to operate one way, the pastor has his or her own understanding of the role, and

2

the congregation has a completely different set of expectations.

Let's look at the local church using the metaphor of a train. The track is what God has called us to do and be as a church. Under the guidance of the Holy Spirit the pastor serves as the conductor, ensuring that the church stays on track and is moving forward purposefully and effectively. But very often the conductor (pastor) becomes distracted or confused and begins to take on tasks and roles that really belong to others. For instance, sometimes the conductor/ pastor gets caught up in managing the daily administration of the train, and steps in to collect, count, and register the tickets. In other cases, the pastor steps in to handle the maintenance and repair of the train, diverting attention to the mechanical, technical, and physical functions of the train itself. Sometimes the pastor erroneously serves as the engineer instead of the conductor. This is when the pastor spends most of his or her time managing the systems and policies of the church. Then there is the baggage-handler pastor, who is trying to do the majority of the ministry in the church instead of identifying and equipping others to serve in ministry. The metaphor breaks down eventually, as all metaphors do, but it is helpful to see all the ways that pastors can get off track. And when we do, it is very easy for congregations to become derailed.

We might refer to the pastor/conductor who has gotten off track as having a crisis of identity. An identity crisis is when a person or perhaps an organization is unclear about what its purpose is and where it is going. The confusion over identity may be a result of wanting to do or be something different, perhaps out of necessity or even misinformation. Regardless of how the crisis came into being, it's important to note that neither a person nor an organization can be what it is created to be until it understands and embraces its true nature. A squirrel can't live as a squirrel if it believes that it is supposed to function like a cat. In the same manner, pastors cannot function as pastors if they believe they are supposed to function as managers. It has been my experience that, by and large, the church is in crisis because of the lack of understanding surrounding the identity of the office of pastor.

Defining the Role of Pastor: Five Essential Functions

Every church and pastor needs to consider—or reconsider—the role of pastor, focusing on the pastor's essential functions. If the pastor is to care for Jesus's sheep, then there are five functions that are, in my view, essential. The pastor must (1) cast a vision, (2) develop staff and leaders around the vision, (3) lead the people, (4) teach and preach, and (5) discern God's will. We will explore these functions further in the following pages, but for now let's briefly unpack each one.

Cast a Vision

For a congregation to effectively make disciples for Jesus Christ, it must know where it is going. They must ask themselves the following questions: Who are the people that we will reach? What must we do in order to reach them? What difference will we make for them, for one another, and for the world on behalf of Christ? How has God uniquely gifted and called us to these specific tasks? These and other questions like them are critical, for they help a congregation discern God's vision for them. The pastor must understand that vision. He must be clear as to what the congregation needs to do in order to effectively practice the Christian ministry. And he or she must communicate that vision, constantly weaving it into the conversation and general mentality of the church. When the pastor consistently communicates a vision of what God is trying to accomplish through a congregation, and how the people will get there, members are given a reason to move forward, to work together, and to move in the same direction toward the same goal. If there is no clear vision, the church never knows if it is on track or not.

4

Develop Staff and Leaders around the Vision

Casting a vision, then, is critical. But what good is vision if no one is able to move toward it? The pastor must equip staff and/or leaders to effectively carry out the vision. It is imperative that the pastor provide tools and resources to help his or her team accurately carry out ministry assignments. That means establishing goals, teaching leadership principles, and building strong and effective teams. Perhaps the most important aspect of developing staff and leaders is for the pastor to help them understand a particular set of leadership values and ethos. When staff and leaders are leading, not only do they represent the church, but also they represent the characteristics and attitudes of the pastor. Without a proper understanding of who the pastor is and what the pastor represents, the leadership team could lead in a way that is contrary to the pastor's principles.

Lead the People

It is important to note that the gift of leadership must be present in order for a person to truly serve as pastor. The pastor must (and *must* might not be a strong enough word) possess the ability to persuade people to follow where he or she leads. Leadership requires that people believe you know where you are going. How can anyone follow you if you are still trying to find your way? There are also other important traits that are critical for pastoral leadership, including integrity, transparency, and compassion. These things are important because people typically don't follow someone they don't trust or someone they don't believe cares about them. If you are to be a leader, you must be willing to care for people.

Teach and Preach

For the pastor, preaching and teaching are the primary tools used to feed God's sheep, explain the vision, and lead the people. Preaching is the pastor's opportunity to share God's vision for the congregation; it is also the time to provide pastoral care, and to nourish the people with the word of God. The Bible is clear that

5

it is the preaching and teaching ministry that will draw people to Jesus, help them to grow in faith, and move them to action. Teaching and preaching provide the pastor occasions to make and strengthen disciples for Jesus Christ.

It is the preaching and teaching ministry that will draw people to Jesus, help them to grow in faith, and move them to action.

Discern God's Will

The last essential of pastoral life is perhaps the greatest because without it, none of the others would be possible. God speaks to us in different ways, and it is of the utmost importance that pastors develop a regular practice of listening to and discerning God's will for the congregation. Without discernment, congregations simply do what they like or what they have always done. That's not who we as people of God are to be. That is true for us as individuals, and it is especially true for us as the church. Knowing how to listen to God and being able to identify God's voice and instructions as they relate to the church is the only way a church can truly be the body of Christ. Whether it is quiet time, searching scripture, fasting, prayer, or journaling, it is vital that pastors be willing and able to listen to and clearly hear the direction God has for the congregation.

When you look at the state of the church in America, especially mainline denominations, it's clear that something is wrong. Church membership and worship attendance have been on the decline for decades. If nothing is done, the church as we know it will cease to exist. Some would even say that soon we will be replaced by rocks that will praise and serve God in a more efficient and effective manner

(Luke 19:40). The problem is not the church itself. After all, Jesus established the church and declared that the gates of hell would not overcome it (Matthew 16:18). The issue at hand is that the church has lost its way to a certain degree. Sure, we still strive to make disciples for Jesus Christ, reach out to those in need, and worship God from week to week. However, the structure for accomplishing this is not as effective as it could be, and one critically weak portion of the structure is the identity of the pastor. We have to reclaim our true role of casting vision, developing leaders, teaching and preaching, leadership, and discerning God's will. We have lost sight of these essentials in the role of pastor; we have allowed our focus to wander, slipping off track.

> # We have to reclaim our true role of casting vision, developing leaders, teaching and preaching, leadership, and discerning God's will.

If the pastor's role is unclear or if the pastor is on the wrong track, then the entire congregation will be on the wrong track. God established the office of pastor so that local congregations would have proper guidance. Without it congregations can become completely derailed.

Ways We Slip Off Track

In my nearly twenty years of ministry, many good Christians have shared with me their expectations of a pastor. Their expectations are, in many cases, based on denominational traditions, congregational needs, American culture, and laity assumptions. It seems that pastors can get off track because they are unprepared, have misguided expectations, take on too many responsibilities, or believe the work of ministry is all theirs to do.

1. New pastors do not fully understand the role, don't know what to expect, or are unprepared.

2. Pastors in new or first-time appointments take the path of least resistance, stepping into the former pastors' shoes and attempting to fulfill the expectations of the congregations, which are based on the former pastors' performances.

3. Pastors buy into a "snowballed" job description, a collection of roles and functions that have been added to by different groups of people, in different settings, over many years. This has resulted in a muddied hodgepodge of roles and expectations, and an impossible and ineffective understanding of the role of pastor.

4. Pastors believe that they alone are truly responsible for the work of ministry. They forget that life in Christ is rooted in community, and that ministry is the work of the people, clergy, leaders, and laity, all together.

A large number of pastors enter the pastorate with some of those same misplaced expectations guiding their ministries. In numerous instances new pastors enter the ministry not knowing what to expect; thus their roles are defined by the parishioners they serve. They are not truly prepared to handle the constant demands of ministry. Pastors are not ready simply because no one has ever told them exactly what a pastor is supposed to do. They simply jump in and begin doing what they see needs to be done rather than what should be done.

In many cases a congregation's understanding of what a pastor should do is based on what the previous pastor did or did not do. This puts the current pastor in a quandary. He or she could set a new course, which could cause dissention, or continue doing what all the former pastors did, which makes everyone happy but goes against what the pastor believes ought to be done. Consider that there are essentials when it comes to pastoring; however, every pastor has different gifts and styles. So when a congregation looks to its new pastor to do what the former pastor did, it may be asking him or her to perform in an area in which he or she is not gifted in. When that happens the present pastor doesn't thrive, and the congregation misses out on the true gifts he or she possesses.

> In many cases a congregation's understanding of what a pastor should do is based on what the previous pastor did or did not do.

For many, the understanding of ministry is based on historical images. Those images have been built upon by each generation. The problem is that it becomes like a lot of worship celebrations I've experienced. In an effort to stay relevant and reach new generations, congregations will sometimes add contemporary components to worship while holding on to what they are already doing. What you end up with is a longer worship celebration that combines the traditional with the contemporary. Furthermore, the worship experience fails to be relevant to anyone because in many instances people don't want a combination; they want more of what they like. Likewise, the Christian church has taken historical images of pastoral ministry and combined them with modern and cultural expectations. All this does is create a job description that is long and unrealistic. The United Methodist theologian Donald Messer puts it this way: "In recent decades more secular models have accented creative dimensions of ministry—counselor, administrator, pastoral director, professional, midwife, player coach, and enabler to name but a few."[1] In essence the pastor has become the church's hired hand to fix all problems and handle all the business of the church.

When you have a bunch of different responsibilities, inevitably some might not get done at all. Because the job duties of the pastor have been added to over the years based on what previous pastors did, the job becomes too much. It's like juggling. Everyone has a limit of how many balls they can juggle. When you pass that limit you begin to drop balls. When you have a too-lengthy pastoral job description, some things don't get done well or at all.

When you have a too-lengthy pastoral job description, some things don't get done well or at all.

I remember early on in ministry when I was serving an aging congregation in the middle of a neighborhood that was completely different demographically from the church members. The congregation was made up of predominantly whites from the baby boomer and builder generations. The surrounding neighborhood was made up of young black families. During my first month serving as pastor, I was asked how I planned to reach the young people in the neighborhood. This was troubling to me because I thought it was the entire congregation's responsibility, not just the pastor's. I could lay out a vision, but we would all have to participate to make it a reality. Apparently we were operating with two very different expectations of the role of the pastor.

Finding Our Way Back

There have been books and seminars focused on explaining how a pastor ought to function in the life of a congregation. If you asked ten people to explain a pastor's function, it is very possible that you would get ten different answers. Today it appears that many are looking at corporate models where the pastor is viewed as the chief executive officer of a small business. If the church is going to be effective, they claim, it must be run like a corporation, with the pastor as head of that corporation. This means the pastor operates as the lead managing director of a congregation. On the other hand, others find using corporate language in the church disturbing. While they still believe the role of the pastor is to manage the congregation, they are uncomfortable using corporate language. So it appears that even the particular words we use to describe the role of a pastor are a point of debate and discussion.

While I believe the church can learn something from the corporate world as it relates to structure and operations, I don't believe the CEO model really does justice to what a pastor has been called to do. A pastor's role is, to a large extent, simpler yet goes deeper and has a longer history than that of CEO. The role of the pastor doesn't need to be reshaped nor does the identity need to be borrowed from the business sector. The role of the pastor is rooted and defined in the Holy Bible. Both the Old and New Testaments give us a clear picture of the purpose of the pastor and provide a basic job description. The role of the pastor is not formulated by a denomination, a congregation's human resources team, or a governing board. It has been prepared by God Almighty and is spelled out within the pages of scripture.

The role of the pastor is not formulated by a denomination, a congregation's human resources team, or a governing board.

I understand that the biblical interpretation of the pastor's role does have to be contextualized for the twenty-first century. The circumstances and culture are immeasurably different today from thousands of years ago. So the practice may look a little different, but the quintessence is the same today as it was in the first century. It is my contention that the nature of the office of pastor is universal and applicable for every age. I believe when the essence of the pastoral role is lived out in accordance with each pastor's context, we will see significant growth, efficiency, effectiveness, and fruitful results in our local congregations.

The Pastor and the People

It is critical that pastors, seminary students, professors, and laity gain an accurate understanding of the office of the pastor if the church is to thrive in the twenty-first century. Current and future pastors need to understand what it is God has called us to do. Not what has always been done in the Western Protestant church but what is the holy mandate of the pastor as it is given by God. We must weed out what have been the historical expectations of pastors and focus on what is supposed to be the role of the pastor according to our understanding of the scriptures. It is also important to include laity in this conversation, as the work of the church is their responsibility, as much or more as it is that of the clergy. It is of little to no benefit to the church if pastors understand their role but the people they serve do not. It is only when pastors and laity understand the role of the pastor that the church as a whole can truly fulfill Christ's call on us.

You can look at it like this: Jesus is the railroad track (after all, he is the Way); the train is the gospel; the church is the passengers; and the pastor is the conductor. In many cases the train has been derailed because the conductor is functioning like a ticket taker. The pastor is acting like a ticket taker because that is the expectation of the passengers. They believe the conductor can and should do both because that's the way it has always been done. The problem is that while the conductor is collecting tickets, the train is drifting off the tracks. That is, the very gospel the church is supposed to proclaim, teach, share, and live out is no longer as meaningful, fruitful, or impactful, not due to faithlessness but because the pastor is spending time and energy away from conducting and spending time and energy in other areas. The gospel and the congregation have gotten off track because the pastor is off track.

In my experience, too many pastors are functioning in a capacity that does not line up with what the office of pastor was designed to do. Our understanding of the role has been shaped by many competing factors, with the biblical job description as one of many. The only way for the local church to truly fulfill its mission is for the pastor's role to be understood and carried out. Every pastor has the same responsibilities and those are not based on a particular congregation or denomination but rooted in the biblical tradition. Congregations and pastors must begin to see how the role of the pastor has been misunderstood and make adjustments. Pastors and congregations who grasp the biblical understanding of the role of pastor and embrace it experience more excitement and energy in worship, in other ministries, and even in commitment to the life and vision of the church.

Questions for Reflection

1. Describe your understanding of the essential functions of the pastor.

2. What or who has most significantly shaped your understanding of the role of the pastor?

3. Where do you look for good models of the pastoral role?

4. What have you understood from the Bible regarding the role of pastor?

5. How does scripture shape the way you live out the role yourself?

Chapter 2
The Need for Change

Don't be conformed to the patterns of this world, but be transformed by the renewing of your minds so that you can figure out what God's will is—what is good and pleasing and mature.

—Romans 12:2

Chugging Along in the Culture

There is an old saying: "If it ain't broke, don't fix it." In other words, if everything is going according to plan, don't change anything. Why mess up a good thing? On the other hand, if things are not going according to plan, why would you want to keep things the same? Why continue doing something that is not working? There's another saying: "If you always do what you've always done, then you'll always get what you've always gotten." As this relates to the church, if the Christian movement in North America is going exactly as we planned, then we should not change anything. However, if things are not going according to plan and congregations are looking for different results, then a change is needed.

It has been well documented that church attendance and participation in North America have experienced a significant decline over the last few decades. The decline is more evident in mainline Protestant congregations. This is not a result of the church losing faith in Jesus. It is more a result of a lack of understanding and direction. There is a lack of clarity about who the pastor is; thus, the congregation is misguided. It is off track.

As church membership grows older, many congregations have not figured out how to reach younger populations. Church membership records are not reflective of church attendance records. A congregation is doing something special if more than 50 percent of its members attend worship each week. It seems almost as if some want their names placed on a membership role just in case God asks someday. This trend of decline in attendance is antithetical to what the church was authorized to do. In the Great Commission, Jesus declared to his followers that they must go and make disciples (Matthew 28:19). Go and not stay, meaning moving beyond the walls of a church house to meet and reach new people. Jesus had the expectation that the church would grow, not decline.

While the church's influence in North America has waned, North American culture is influencing the entire world. One quick example of this is hip-hop. Hip-hop (not just rap music but the language, dress, and ideology associated with the music) started on the streets of New York City and can now be seen and heard on just about every continent. Can our culture and church coexist in harmony or will there always be tension and competition?

The question could be asked, and rightfully so, if American culture has overwhelmed the church. This is not a question that is exclusive to the twenty-first century. This question was the premise of German theologian H. Richard Niebuhr's book *Christ and Culture*. It was Niebuhr's contention that Christ and popular culture seem to contradict each other. For those of us who follow Christ, this is problematic because the church should have a positive impact on culture. It seems, at least to me, that we are losing that battle. Niebuhr contends that Christ, through his church, should transform culture. That is not happening in North America today. Our culture has experienced a great shift, and there appears to be a complete disregard for what the church is doing. For families in North

America today, many activities are planned on Sunday mornings, placing attractive options in direct competition with worship plans. At one point in American history, the church was the only game in town on Sunday morning. In most communities, people either went to worship or stayed at home. During this period the church did not have to work hard to draw members. Churchgoing and even active involvement in church were ingrained, a part of North American culture. Today, there are department store sales, professional sports, and much more taking place on Sunday. Perhaps the most prevalent and fast-growing activity is the sports games on Sundays. When I grew up we played Little League games on Saturdays and went to church on Sundays. Today, several families and children at St. James regularly miss Sunday morning because they are participating in soccer and basketball tournaments.

In the midst of this great cultural shift, the church has just continued chugging along, seemingly unaware of the dramatic changes in the landscape all around it. And in our state of unawareness (or ignorance or delusion), we have slipped off track.

And few in the culture around us seem to care—or even to notice. We are witnessing a decrease in the church's influence and impact on American culture. For many people today the church is just another organization. Others view the church as irrelevant and outdated in its practices and beliefs. Pastors are often viewed by those outside of the church as the persons in society tasked with conducting funerals and weddings. Beyond that, people aren't sure what a pastor does all week. Most of us pastors have been asked at one time or another, "What is it that you do all week?" We pastors typically put in about two days' worth of work each week, right? That's the perception shared by many unchurched people and even some regular churchgoers. We put our sermons together on Saturday evenings and then preach on Sunday mornings. We have the rest of the week off unless someone is in the hospital or there is a funeral.

Most of us pastors have been asked at one time or another, "What is it that you do all week?"

I remember hearing a sermon illustration about a tornado hitting a small town. Fortunately, the tornado did not do much damage to the town. The local paper reported the town's circumstances on the front page. The headline read "Thank God, only the church was destroyed." It appears today that for many the church house is just another building in the community. It's something more, perhaps, for a select few people.

It is interesting and perhaps instructive to note that in the midst of this crisis in the North American church, Christianity is spreading rapidly on the continents of Africa and South America. African and South American congregations are growing because they are certain of what they've been called to do. Their purpose has not become diluted or muddied or patched over with add-ons and extraneous expectations. They understand the Great Commission and structure their congregations in a manner to fulfill the commission. They are focused, and in this regard they are on track. But these congregations do have advantages that we do not. One key advantage, although it may not seem like one, is that they don't have the land, facilities, equipment, or infrastructure that we do. This certainly works to their disadvantage in many ways, but it does allow these churches to focus on reaching people for Christ.

In North America we spend an extraordinary amount of time and energy trying to manage what we have. We have budgets to meet, buildings to maintain, programs to operate, and members to keep satisfied. And our North American culture has come to value *appearances*, literally, more than nearly anything else. We value big things, shiny things, new things. This shift of values has influenced the church and the expectations of our congregants and the people in our communities. In part to keep up appearances, pastors often concentrate on these areas rather than on true pastoring. Over time, the pastor is, in effect, just spinning her or his wheels, maintaining the engine rather than moving the congregation forward. Thus, many churches remain in the same place on the track today as thirty years ago. It is important to note that we must be good stewards of church resources, and that excellence is a standard worth striving for. But we must also question and honestly evaluate our Christ-shaped needs versus our culturally shaped wants. Jesus intended for congregations to thrive and *go*—but this will happen only when pastors focus on the things they were commissioned to do.

We must question and honestly evaluate our Christ-shaped needs versus our culturally shaped wants.

Letting Go of the Past: Pastor as Administrator

It is also interesting and instructive to consider a way we pastors might be clinging to the cultural landscape we've long since passed, refusing to see the new opportunities around us. The pastor serving as the chief manager and ministry administrator may be a model that worked effectively at one time, in some churches. But it is not the best model for the twenty-first century, and it is not a biblical model for pastoral ministry.

Soon after finishing their seminary training, most pastors discover that they did not learn how to manage a congregation. Seminaries teach biblical interpretation, homiletics, and theological discourse but do not teach about budgets, facility management, or organizational supervision. The pastor must learn these skills on the job. It is easy to see how this can be damaging to the growth of the congregation, as the pastor spends time and energy on learning by trial and error how to be the administrative officer of an organization, rather than on all those other valuable endeavors we learned about in seminary.

Soon after finishing their seminary training, most pastors discover that they did not learn how to manage a congregation.

One might argue that if pastors aren't learning those things in seminary, then why don't seminaries make those subjects a part of the curriculum? On the surface this seems like an easy solution. It is my contention that if seminaries placed more emphasis on teaching management and administration, they would produce great executives but not great pastors. It's not so much that seminaries need to change their curriculum as that congregations and pastors need to reshape their understanding of the role of the pastor.

This pastor-as-administrator form of ministry can cause burnout and ineffectiveness. When the pastor's key function is being chief manager, he or she must make sure that everything is operating properly, ensuring that all the cylinders are oiled and clicking. This has become such an issue that I've heard many pastors say they wish they had gone to business school. That would be great training, but it would not help the person become a better pastor; it would only help him become a better businessman. Knowing how to manage and operate a church does not make a person a good shepherd for the Lord. Those are two different things.

I've seen how the administrator model creates an ineffective pastor. Several years ago I made a rare visit to another church on a Sunday morning. The pastor of the church invited me to his office, where he was supposed to be centering himself and making final preparations for the worship experience and his sermon. As we sat in his office, with the minutes ticking down to the start of worship, members kept coming into his office to ask questions about all sorts of details related to the worship experience. These people needed very specific instructions about what they were to do, and what was supposed to take place in the fast-approaching worship service. The more this pastor answered questions and directed his parishioners, the less time he was able to spend on preparing his mind and soul for preaching. And I wondered if the interruptions might be having an even more negative effect by causing him to tire before even stepping into the sanctuary. Going back and forth with parishioners is sometimes exhausting and can easily drain even the most energetic and gregarious pastor. This sort of situation is a problem for us as pastors. Preaching is one of our essential roles! It is the primary way in which people receive a word from the Lord. The pastor and his congregation misunderstood the pastor's main function on that Sunday morning. They were all off track.

For too long, too many people have viewed the pastor as the administrator, expecting her or him to have all the answers and to be a part of every decision. Consequently, the pastor feels as though she or he must possess detailed knowledge of the intricacies of church operations and ministries. A great deal of the pastor's time is spent ensuring that she or he knows what's going on, where it is taking place, and getting directly involved in every aspect of church life. A good friend of mine used to work at home during the week rather than at the church house because of the constant questions he received regarding what was going on at the church: "Pastor, what time is the revival this week?"; "Pastor, what kind of copier should we get?"; "Can the homeowners' association use our building on Thursday?" While these are important questions, they are not the sorts of questions most pastors should be addressing. Unfortunately, this paradigm has led us to refer to the pastor's study as the pastor's office. There is a difference. An office is where business takes place, but a study is where prayer, reading, writing, and planning take place.

To use another analogy, it is as if the pastor serves as the church mechanic and is responsible for keeping all the church parts in working order. Every time a part doesn't seem to be working properly, the pastor is called in to fix it. If something needs to be repaired, refined, or replaced, the pastor/mechanic must directly, immediately, and personally address the problem. It is important to say that this routine is not solely the fault of the laity. It's not just a matter of misplaced congregational expectations. Often pastors want to have a hand in every aspect of congregational life. Because they've never been told otherwise, they believe that is what a pastor is supposed to do. They place "administration" on the list of essential functions, where it does not belong. And, unfortunately for the congregation, if the pastor is serving as the go-to person for every administrative problem, that means she or he is not serving as the God-appointed pastor in the truest sense of the office.

If the pastor is enmeshed in day-to-day details of *what is going on* in the church, then there is probably precious little time for the pastor to consider *where the church is going*. In today's culture, more than ever, people want to know: What's next? Where are we going? What is the vision we are being called to pursue, and what difference will it make in the world? Church operations and administration are critical. But they do not represent an essential function of the role of pastor. Someone needs to focus on leading the congregation into the future.

Church operations and administration are critical. But they do not represent an essential function of the role of pastor.

22

Pastors who function in this administrator model become embroiled in matters that are *not essential* functions of the role of pastor. The people become passive consumers of a commodity that is dished up for them each week, rather than forward-moving, kingdom-building, faith-sharing Christians. And eventually the church stalls or even begins to roll backward on the track. Congregations can rely on the pastor so much that they can't eat a church meal until the pastor comes and blesses the food.

Learning from the Current Landscape: Look Forward

Finally, in this examination of how we relate to the cultural landscape, let's consider a way we should learn from the current terrain. We live in an age where things change rapidly and the new can become old very fast. The technology of cell phones, computers, laptops, tablets, and televisions is constantly advancing, and people look forward to each innovation. There is a great deal of excitement in the air when something new is about to hit the market. Steve Jobs, the late cofounder and former CEO of Apple, was always looking forward to what was next. Jobs seemed to never be satisfied, and he did not become complacent with the success of the latest products. He knew that people would remain excited about a product for only so long. Eventually, they would want to know what was next. That's why he always thought ahead. Steve Jobs understood that he needed to continually look forward. He let the world know, "If you like what we have right now, just wait, there is more to come—and it will be even better and more exciting than what you already have." And guess what? The world waited in great anticipation.

If the church is going to fulfill its God-given purpose, to grow numerically and in effectiveness, pastors must constantly look ahead. We can't become satisfied with our past accomplishments. It is important for pastors and congregations to celebrate together the church's milestones and successes. But if we simply celebrate where we are and work to keep everything running smoothly so that we can stay there, we have failed.

Questions for Reflection

1. What do you see as the biggest cultural threat to the local congregations in your community?

2. What are the advantages and disadvantages of viewing the pastor as a CEO?

3. How might your ministry change if you were to focus on the essentials? In what ways might this allow you to be a more effective leader?

4. How much time during an average month do you spend on management and administration?

5. What biblical examples of leadership resonate most strongly with you—a leader (or leaders) who communicated God's vision of the future and of a path forward for God's people? What do you learn from this leader's example? How might you apply these lessons in your own ministry setting?

Chapter 3
Essential: Cast the Vision

When there's no vision, the people get out of control,
but whoever obeys instruction is happy.

—*Proverbs 29:18*

Before we go any further, I believe it is important to address one of the major struggles for pastors in the twenty-first century. If this struggle is not addressed, there is no time to understand or articulate a vision for the congregation. The challenge has to do with a question: Is a pastor a leader or a manager? And another question: What's the difference between a leader and a manager? Managing will produce one thing, while leading will produce something entirely different. I want to take some time discussing what a pastor is, what the difference between a pastor and a manager is, and why it matters. Too many pastors spend an enormous amount of time managing rather than leading. There is a huge difference between the two. I believe one leads to congregational excellence, while the other can lead to complacency, stagnation, and decline. What prevents many congregations from effectively making disciples for Jesus Christ is that neither pastors nor congregations understand the role of the pastor. The current typical understanding of a pastor's role is more cultural than biblical. As we discussed in the last chapter, the role of the pastor is often based on the outdated concept of pastor as church administrator. Many pastors and parishioners believe the pastor is responsible for handling the day-to-day operations of the congregation. But managing/administrating is not one of the essential functions of the pastor.

I was recently at a conference with lay and clergy, and I heard this statement: "My pastor is a great teacher, but he does not know how to manage." Although I had never met the lady's pastor, I believed her. I wanted to tell her, "Your pastor did not go to seminary to learn how to *manage* the church. He went to school to learn how to *lead* the church. He spent time and effort and resources to attend seminary so that he could effectively and accurately communicate the gospel message."

The reason so many Christians in the twenty-first century look at a pastor as a manger can probably be traced back to the institutionalization of the church. Now, I am in no way against the church as an institution. As an institution the church is able to effect change and make a difference all over the world. The church is able to build schools, hospitals, universities, homeless shelters, and so much more because it is established and organized with structures, processes, rules, and traditions. However, with the institutionalization of the church, several things have happened over the centuries that have led to the misunderstanding of the role of the pastor. One critical example is the church's decline in acknowledging and employing its spiritual gifts. John Wesley accredited the decline in the practice of spiritual gifts not to their being unavailable but to the spiritual decay of the church. This decline shifted the pastoral focus from leading to managing.[1] Let us examine this claim and its significance for us as pastors today.

Spirit-Led vs. Pastor-Managed

The apostles Paul and Peter talk candidly about the gifts of the Spirit in the New Testament. Through their writings in Romans, Corinthians, Ephesians, and Peter, we learn that the gifts of the Spirit are available for all believers. However, as the church continued to grow in the first century, there was more of a need to establish protocol by way of instituting certain offices in the church. The author of Ephesians declares that God has given gifts to the church in the form of apostles, prophets, evangelists, pastors, and teachers (Ephesians 4:11). These persons, set aside for vocational ministry, had the responsibility of equipping "God's people for the work of serving and building up the body of Christ" (Ephesians 4:12). This marks a transition in the Christian movement when there became a clear distinction between clergy and laity.

The office of pastor is meant to be *a gift to the church*, whereas laity are given gifts *for the sake of the church.*

Unfortunately, the establishment of vocational ministers may have led to the lack of awareness and application of spiritual gifts. Once vocational offices for the church were put in place, laity may have been less inclined to participate in ministry, believing it was the responsibility of bishops and pastors. Thus, pastors began to handle the bulk of administration, hands-on ministry, and the overall operation of the church. And, as we have discussed, this is still a prevalent model today. Facing competing demands for time and attention, pastors began neglecting the spiritual gifts God had placed in them as a gift to the church. The office of pastor is meant to be *a gift to the church*, whereas laity are given gifts *for the sake of the church.* The pastor is a gift to the church because that office is responsible for casting the vision, developing staff and leaders, teaching and preaching, leading the people, and discerning God's will for the congregation. The decline in spiritual gifts activity was so apparent that the great Reformer Martin Luther implied the necessity of gifts as he related the priesthood of all believers to spiritual gifts. The fact that Martin Luther, back in the sixteenth century, felt the need to express that all believers have roles to play in doing ministry indicates that such thought was not normal. It's almost as if laity did not practice ministry as much as they were the beneficiaries of ministry from clergy. The fact of the matter is that clergy were and still are viewed as the ones who are supposed to be the primary ministry workers in the church. This misunderstanding has drawn pastors away from doing what the Apostle Paul declares is the role of vocational ministers— "to equip God's people for the work of serving and building up the body of Christ" (Ephesians 4:12).

Equipping the People for Ministry

As clergy we sometimes don't empower laity for ministry because we do not trust that they can handle it. After all, they are volunteers without the calling and the proper education to carry out the weightier issues of ministry. I have a friend in ministry in a growing congregation. She has been handling the hospital visits for years on her own. Now, as the congregation has grown, she has a hard time turning some of the responsibilities over to a team of lay volunteers. Her rationale is that when there is a crisis in someone's life the pastor should respond, not laity. She reasons that most laity are not equipped to handle those situations. She is correct; most people are not equipped for ministry. An essential function of our job is to equip them! Equipping comes by way of developing the staff and leadership but mostly through the preaching and teaching ministry of the pastor. If laity can't do the job, it is because pastors are not equipping them to do so.

Leading vs. Managing

Many people view the pastor as chief executive officer, and certainly the pastor has a role in overseeing the affairs of the church.

Some will say that the pastor is the chief executive fund-raiser. Indeed, the pastor has the responsibility of helping to raise awareness about the importance of giving to God's church. But at its core, the pastor's role is not fund-raising. Rather, it is casting the vision so that people know why they are giving and so they understand what can and will be accomplished through their giving. To be sure, the oversight that a pastor provides has to do more with leading than managing. I'm reminded of 1 Timothy 5:17, where Paul talks about the elder leading the affairs of the church not managing the affairs. What is the difference? Managing means taking care of what is already in place. It involves ensuring that programs are running properly, the people are in the right positions, finances are handled properly, facilities are kept in order, and the overall administration of the church is flowing efficiently and effectively. In short, to once again use an automobile metaphor, making sure all cylinders are oiled and functioning correctly. The problem with this is that if a pastor spends all available time taking care of what is already in place, then very little time can be spent planning for the future.

> If a pastor spends all available time taking care of what is already in place, then very little time can be spent planning for the future.

I remember one time when a visiting pastor and I were sitting in my study chatting. I am not sure how we got on the subject, but he asked me where we got our office supplies. I responded that I didn't know and would have to ask the operations managers. I could tell that he was a little angry and surprised by my answer because he asked, "How can the pastor not know the details of his church?" My contention was and is that I was not hired to make sure the church had office supplies. I was hired to preach, teach, lead the people (in worship and sacraments), develop staff and leaders, discern God's direction, and cast the vision. It might be helpful if pastors think of it like this: Would the congregation rather I spend my time praying and studying or meeting with suppliers, contractors, and accountants? I would imagine that most congregants would prefer the former and not the latter.

Management should be only a small portion of what the pastor does. It is important that the operations of the church are handled well. That's why pastors should ensure that the right people are in place to handle those things. Those persons have to be held accountable whether they are paid or volunteers. The pastor's job is leading, meaning communicating what's next and where the church is going; in other words, casting the vision. Leading also means presiding over the worship and sacraments. Because worship and the sacraments of the church are vital for a congregation's well-being and growth, it is necessary for the pastor to supervise these routine practices. Furthermore, this means the pastor must make sure that those who oversee the operations of the church understand the vision and their role in accomplishing it.

Leading with Vision

Moses, while leading the people to a new life after leaving Egypt, had to be educated concerning his true role. Jethro, Moses's father-in-law, informed Moses that he was spending too much time managing people and trying to fix every issue. Jethro, in his wisdom, told Moses to get some people on his team who were trustworthy and loved the Lord and empower them to manage the smaller situations in the community. Jethro shared with Moses that he ought to deal with only the major concerns among the people. You see, Jethro was able to get Moses to understand that if Moses spent all of his energy on all the minor issues, he could easily lose focus on the larger picture, which was leading the people through the wilderness and eventually to the Promised Land.

In order for Moses to properly lead the people during this period of transition, he could not supervise and personally care for every person, tribe, or issue. His task was to continue to keep in front of the people the vision God had given him. Casting the vision and teaching how to reach the vision was Moses's primary responsibility. Let me now try to summarize Moses's leadership style as an example of spending more time leading and less time managing.

Leading as Moses Led

Let me begin by stating that one of the most fundamental elements of any successful organization is leadership. However, it is also one of the most misunderstood qualities as it relates to congregational development and structure. We are in the midst of a drastic shift within many mainline churches (some would say the shift has already taken place), in that membership is declining, the impact of the church on society is questioned, and effective leadership is a rarity. Perhaps the reason for the deterioration of many churches is a result of a misunderstanding of what leadership is and what it is not. If the church is to reverse this trend, leaders must come to the realization that true leadership means guiding people into the vision that God has for them, individually and collectively. Lovett Weems's book *Church Leadership* has helped me develop my theology of leadership.[2]

Leader vs. Boss: Sell the Vision

First, it is essential to differentiate between being a leader and being a boss. A boss has authority and power based on his or her position. A boss tells people what they are supposed to do, and people do it because there are consequences for disobeying. A leader, on the other hand, may have authority based on position; however, a leader does not have the luxury (depending on how you look at it) of telling people what to do. People don't have to do what a leader tells them to do. Therefore, a leader has to convince people that what they are doing and where they are going are in the best interests of the group. Our congregations are made up of leaders, not bosses, and we have to persuade people to follow us.

Our congregations are made up of leaders, not bosses, and we have to persuade people to follow us.

This was the case with Moses as he had to convince the Hebrew people to leave Egypt. He did not have the power or the authority to make them leave; he had to convince them that they should leave. It began with a vision. Moses explained to the people that it was time to claim what God had promised Abraham, Isaac, and Jacob: a land of their own. Where they were going and why it was better than their current situation became clear, and that's why the people followed the leadership of Moses.

Understand the People

Second, since a church is made up of several members, success depends on team effort. Moreover, because a church consists of many individuals who come together to work as one, each church will have its own way of doing things. The language, style, and images of a church are important aspects that must be taken into consideration if a pastor is going to effectively lead a congregation. What is a perfect goal for one church might be completely unrealistic and irrelevant to another. Thus, if a pastor is to motivate and draw the cooperation of the parishioners, she or he must understand the ethos of the people.

Once the pastor understands the culture of the congregation, he or she will be able to help shape and mold a vision that is relevant and acceptable. The pastor must be sure to continuously keep the vision before the people and help them understand its importance to the point that it becomes the natural definition of who the people are and what they are called to do. The acceptability and relevance of the vision can make or break the vision becoming a reality. I doubt very much that Moses alone could have led a group of Egyptians out into the wilderness. The Promised Land was not a part of Egyptian culture, so traveling to Canaan under harsh conditions would not have been relevant to them. Shaping, articulating, and embracing the vision in a culturally relevant way is one of the most important roles of any leader, regardless of the organization.

Establish Supportive Teams

It is my belief that even with a dynamic vision and a clear plan, it is impossible to reach the vision without the right support. Moses's father-in-law understood that Moses would not be able to success-fully lead the Hebrews without a strong support system in place. Moses built a team of leaders who shared the same values. More importantly, Moses's support team had a connection with the same God. No matter how gifted an individual is, if that individual doesn't share the same values, beliefs, and culture as the leader, excellence should not be expected in that ministry. It is my contention that it is better to have a committed team that understands and accepts the vision, the values, and the beliefs of the pastor than it is to have a league of extraordinarily gifted individuals who don't value the same things. Leadership team members must be on the same page; other-wise, those you intend to lead will see the disunity, and if the leader-ship is not united then the congregation will not be united.

Cultivate a Deep Prayer Life

Not only did Moses present a clear picture to the people of where they were going, but also the people believed that God was with Moses. When it comes to church leadership, it is imperative that the people understand that God is truly speaking to and through the leader. Otherwise, the vision becomes merely an idea that the pastor is trying to push off on the parishioners. The perceived rela-tionship that the pastor has with God will determine whether or not parishioners are willing to follow. That's why it is essential for the pastor to have a deep prayer life. Without a meaningful prayer life, there can be no true leadership or vision in God's church.

The book of Exodus clearly says that Moses got away from everyone to spend time alone with God on Mount Sinai. His alone time with God provided him with the vision, the strength, and the courage to lead the Hebrew people during their wilderness experience. Spending time with God is not just for the personal faith development of the pastor but for the entire congregation. As the pastor grows in faith through prayer time, the entire congregation benefits because they are exposed to God through the pastor. When Moses came down from the mountaintop, the people could see the glory of the Lord in him. It's the same with the pastor. People can tell when their leader has been spending time with the Lord because it shows up in the pastor's preaching, teaching, and interactions with others. Spending quality time with God is imperative when it comes to leadership in our local congregations.

I believe our local congregations would thrive if pastors took notice of Moses's leadership style. Sure, Moses had his challenges, but it is pretty remarkable that he was able to get this huge congregation to follow him in the midst of uncertainty, duress, and chaos. In spite of all the seemingly insurmountable circumstances that Moses faced, he led the people successfully because he sold the vision, understood the people, developed a strong team, and spent quality time alone with God.

If the vision is not laid out, the congregation will remain in the exact same position. That might sound good if your congregation is currently thriving; however, seasons change, and what you do right now will not always be relevant and applicable. Just ask the inventors of the Polaroid camera, vinyl records, and VHS tape. The world around us is constantly changing, and the church must change as well. Our core values and beliefs remain constant, but we must change the way we do things if we are to remain relevant in the twenty-first century.

Many congregations have trouble reaching new people for Jesus

34

Christ because the pastor and church leaders don't understand their roles. Once congregations are established and have a budget, a strong membership, property, and ministries, pastors tend to focus on how to maintain all of those things. Perhaps it is simply our human nature to preserve what we have, first and foremost. We tell ourselves, "We have what we need, which is good. We don't want to lose it. So we must hold on to the members, facilities, and ministries that we have in place now." When pastors and congregations go into this care-and-preserve mode, they are no longer outwardly focused but rather inwardly focused. This is generally the beginning of a congregation's decline.

Caring for the People

Part of the struggle for congregations is the desire for the pastor to focus on care of the members. They want more general face time with the senior pastor, and of course they want to be visited if they are in the hospital. In most congregations, if the pastor allots half of his time to direct congregational care, other essential functions will be neglected. These include teaching and preaching, leading the people, developing staff and leaders, visioning, and discerning God's will. Congregational care is one of the essential functions of pastoral ministry. It is also, however, a function that can override other essential functions, because the time required is seemingly without limit. This is especially true for pastors in large congregations.

In most congregations, if the pastor allots half of his time to direct congregational care, other essential functions will be neglected.

Congregational care is extremely important when it comes to the vitality of a church. The pastor of a large and growing church may

35

not have time to be at the center of congregational care. But this does not mean the pastor is uninvolved or unconcerned. Many churches operate several different ministries that serve as congregational care ministries, each approaching a different set of needs or a different population within the church. Examples are ministries of care and nurture, bereavement ministries, Stephen ministries, eldercare ministries, and visitation ministries. In some large church settings, these ministries and their staff and laity serve as the agents of the pastor in fulfilling the essential pastoral function of caring for the people. In some churches, staff persons are hired and laity are equipped exclusively for this purpose. This can be an effective model, especially in places where the burdens, struggles, sins, and concerns of people are growing and changing all the time. In fulfilling this essential function, pastors of large churches must be careful and creative, or they may find themselves slipping off track in a new way, neglecting the other essential functions of ministry.

It might be possible, I suppose, to conclude from the preceding paragraphs that I am asserting that the management of ministries is relatively unimportant or that in some churches congregational care can be left to chance. But I am suggesting neither of those things. Good management and congregational care are both extremely important for the vitality of the congregation. What I am suggesting is that like Moses, we pastors are to appoint, equip, and empower trustworthy men and women (paid or unpaid, depending on the church size and budget) to oversee the management of and, in some cases, the congregational care for the church. The pastor, like Moses, must always focus on the larger picture. Constantly casting the vision and teaching the people how to move toward that vision is the pastor's job. Lovett Weems has written and taught about the fact that leaders must do what only they can do—leave to others what others can do, and focus on the things that will happen only if the leader does them. Vision is one of those things. No one else in the church will cast the vision, nor should they. This is something that only you as the pastor can do, so you must not shrink from it.[3]

Moving Off the Mountaintop

Again like Moses, the pastor can never be satisfied with the current position of the congregation. Jesus himself addressed the issue of remaining stagnant. Jesus, Peter, James, and John went off together, and Jesus was transfigured before their eyes on the mountaintop. Standing next to Jesus were Moses and Elijah. Here we had Moses the lawgiver and Elijah the great prophet. Jesus stood between them as the embodiment and fulfillment of the Law and the Prophets. The disciples were so thrilled that they wanted to set up three tents and remain right there on the mountain. Who could blame them—they were in a great place, in the presence of holiness. Jesus, however, said, "We cannot stay here." Jesus understood why they wanted to stay. Those three apostles had everything they needed; in that moment, life could not be any better or more fulfilling or utterly amazing for the three of them. But Jesus was not just thinking about Peter, James, and John. He was thinking of all the people down in the valleys, across the land, the "others" everywhere. Jesus and the three disciples could not stay where they were because there was much more work to be done.

Many congregations are like those apostles. Congregations over time reach a place where they are comfortable with what's going on and want to remain right there. The challenging news is that unless everyone in the world has a relationship with Jesus, until there are no more homeless people and there is no more hunger, violence, or injustice, *"You can't stay there!"*

That illustrates the difference between a leader and a manager. The manager's job is to take care of what's in place. She or he is not really concerned with where we need to go. The primary task is to make sure that what we have is cared for properly. The leader's primary responsibility is to look at the current situation—to peer out the train windows at the landscape around us—and to envision with God where we ought to go. Throughout scripture we see God trying to move God's people from one place to a better place, a place where there is something more or something new to do. God moved Abram from the land of Ur, his homeland, to the land of Canaan.

God moved the children of Israel from Egyptian bondage to a better place—the land of promise. God through Jesus went from a poor town called Nazareth to the cross on Calvary. Jesus went from the grave to glory. God's intent for God's people has never been that they remain where they are but rather that they move on to a better place. That's the role of the pastor, to lead the congregation from one place to the new place God has in store for them.

The leader's primary responsibility is to look at the current situation—to peer out the train windows at the landscape around us—and to envision with God where we ought to go.

Scripture also offers a beautiful and helpful metaphor for this visionary leading that we pastors are called to do. Let's divert from our train-and-track metaphor briefly to consider our role as the *shepherd*. The words for *pastor* in Greek and Hebrew are the same words for *shepherd*. This literal meaning of the word *pastor* has been applied metaphorically to Christian ministers as a symbol of their role. Examining what shepherds did in biblical times will help us understand this chapter's key point from another, larger perspective.

In 1 Samuel 17, when David was sharing his résumé with King Saul in an effort to explain why he was qualified to take on Goliath, he talked about his time as a shepherd. David explained that when the sheep were under attack from a lion or bear, he rescued the sheep. The only way for David to know when one of the sheep was under attack was to keep his eyes on all the sheep. If he gave all his attention to one, two, or a small group of sheep, he might not notice when a lion snatched up another sheep that was not part of the group he was focused on. Furthermore, it would have been the shepherd's job to lead the sheep away from harm. In essence that's what the pastor must do: make sure he or she is watching out for and looking over the entire congregation, not just a few members. A pastor must provide individual care when needed and lead the congregation out of and through difficult times and issues.

In this chapter we have explored how the pastor is to function as a leader, not as a manager. The imagery of the shepherd presented in Psalm 23 makes it clear that a shepherd's most critical job is to lead. This foundational psalm does not make reference to the shepherd's managing anything. Yet, we do see the word *leads* mentioned. David writes, "The LORD is my shepherd. I lack nothing. He lets me rest in grassy meadows; he leads me to restful waters" (Psalm 23:1-2). David is not in want because he knows that God as shepherd will lead him where he needs to go. Sheep don't spend their time worrying about where to go; that is the shepherd's job. David is not in want because the shepherd foresees his needs. The shepherd has a clear vision.

This is exactly what a pastor is called to do. The pastor is called to lead God's sheep to green pastures so they can eat. It is very important for the pastor to also understand that although the sheep may be eating grass and enjoying life, they cannot stay there. The reason they should not get too comfortable is because the longer they stay in one pasture, the more grass they eat. Every strand of grass they eat moves them closer and closer to running out of food. Thus, the pastor must always be thinking ahead. The pastor must constantly be looking for the next pasture of green grass so that the sheep always have something to eat. Too often congregations are so satisfied with their current worship program, educational program, structure, and ministries that they want to just stay put, enjoying the great life on that mountaintop—or at least the familiar life of their good old church. They don't want to move or to change a thing. Sometimes pastors also want to remain, because they don't want to rock the boat.

But eventually things become bland and monotonous. The

pasture wears thin, food runs out, and the sheep begin straying, looking for other congregations or other activities where they can be fed something new and fresh. The pastor has failed to see beyond the pasture gates and has failed to lead the sheep.

George Bullard, in "The Life Cycle and Stages of Congregational Development," suggests that without re-visioning and restructuring, at some point a congregation will die.[4] He believes the best time to re-vision and restructure is when a congregation is in its prime, because that's when a congregation still has resources and energy to make the shift. If the redevelopment of the congregation does not happen at the right time, the transition becomes harder because the congregational numbers are smaller, resources are fewer, and the members are older. Therefore, it becomes critical, in my estimation, that pastors be willing to rock the boat for the sake of congregational survival. It's not easy, nor is it fun, but neither is trying to get sheep to leave a pasture where they have been eating for some time.

This metaphor reveals a few other lessons for us as pastors. Here we see that leadership does not mean showing each sheep where to stand, or dividing them into particular groups, or standing over them, instructing them when and how to eat, or telling them how much to eat. Leadership from this pastoral perspective means to celebrate the fact that with God's help you are leading the sheep to a great place. But it also means you understand that the place will sustain the sheep for only so long. This is perhaps why many church members leave a congregation after so many years of membership. The church has been in the same place for a long time, and the food is running out. It was great in the beginning, but now the people want something new, something more. The place of faith development that once nurtured people along in their spiritual journey has now become repetitive. The organizational structure that once helped the church grow no longer works. The ministries that were once engaging seem to have lost steam. The worship that was once full of creativity and innovation has now become flat and predictable. The pastor must not stay planted inside the gates, content to stay put. We cannot stay here! The pastor must first prepare and then lead the people to the next green pasture.

40

Questions for Reflection

1. What could your congregation do to help shift the role of pastor from managing to leading?

2. What would it mean for your congregation if you were to focus on equipping people and the laity doing ministry? What would be the likely positive and negative consequences?

3. Is it reasonable to expect pastors to delegate the responsibility of management to others? Why or why not?

4. Consider the roles of pastor and boss. In your experience, do these roles conflict with each other? How?

5. What would it take to begin shifting your congregation toward the process of re-visioning and transition?

Chapter 4

Essential: Lead the People

Then the LORD told me: Get going. Lead the people so they can enter and take possession of the land that I promised I'd give to their ancestors.
—*Deuteronomy 10:11*

The Risk of Leading into Uncharted Territory

There is a process that lobsters experience called molting. This is when they outgrow and must leave their shells and develop new ones. If the lobster refuses to the leave the shell it will die, because the shell is simply too small. Once the lobster leaves that shell, it is vulnerable and has no protection from predators or hard surfaces that can cause harm. The lobster has a choice: remain in the shell that is too small and die or leave what it has been accustomed to with the hope of developing something bigger, stronger, and better. The same is true with congregations. Sometimes we must be willing to leave the comfort of what we are used to and explore something bigger, stronger, and better. If we refuse to change and decide to remain exactly where we are, our fate will be similar to that of a lobster that refuses to leave the shell it has outgrown.

Jesus was referring to the Gentiles when he made this profound statement: "I have other sheep that don't belong to this sheep pen. I

43

must lead them too. They will listen to my voice and there will be one flock, with one shepherd" (John 10:16). Jesus wanted his successors (his disciples) to make sure that they shared the gospel with those who were outside the house of Jacob. For most of the followers of Jesus, this would be problematic, because they did not know how to reach the Gentiles. They were unfamiliar with the Gentile culture and even despised it to a certain degree. Nevertheless, as leaders of the church, they were called to reach those who were different from themselves. The Apostle Paul would eventually emerge as the perfect candidate to take the gospel message to the Gentiles. Paul was well versed in Jewish tradition and scripture. He was also familiar with Greco-Roman philosophy and culture and was in fact a Roman citizen. Thus, Paul was able to lead the Christian church into new and uncharted territory.

I believe pastors are called to do the same. In order to lead the church into new and uncharted territory, the pastor must avoid the tendency to function as church manager and live into the essential role of leader. She or he must ask the question, "Where is God calling our congregation to go next?" It would have been easy for the Apostle Paul to stay right there in Jerusalem, where there were already Christians, to spiritually nurture that flock. But what would have been the result? The local church in Jerusalem would not have grown, and Jesus's call might not have begun to be fulfilled. Christianity would not be the global religion it is today. But Paul had the foresight to minister outside of Jerusalem and beyond the Jewish people. Paul understood that to remain in Jerusalem would have stifled the gospel movement by keeping the gospel in one place and thus reaching no one new. In similar fashion, we pastors need to adopt a Pauline mentality in leading our congregations to go beyond where we are to reach new people for Christ. I would go so far as to say that if the church is not looking to reach new people, then either the pastor or the congregation, or perhaps both, is off track.

The Gentiles of the twenty-first century are young adults. This group seems to be absent from many of our congregations on Sunday morning. In order for pastors to lead their congregations into this new Gentile (young adult) territory, it is vital for us to accept a serious flaw that is prevalent in many of our congregations: our belief that if we keep doing what we have been doing and simply extend an invitation to young adults, they will come. That is simply not the case.

A friend of mine invited me to go fishing with him. I'm not a fisherman, but in an effort to show that I was not clueless, I brought my own equipment. My friend used crickets and worms as bait; I used French fries. The reason I used French fries is because I love French fries. At the end of the day my friend had caught a bunch of fish. I'd caught none. I asked him, "Why did you catch so many while I caught none?" He replied, "Because you were using bait that *you* like, and I was using bait that *they* like."

That is precisely how the North American church, as a whole, has acted when it comes to reaching young adults. We want to use the bait that we like instead of using methods and practices that speak directly to them. How is it that pastors can lead congregations to reach new people, specifically young adults? Part of a pastor's job is to understand the terrain over which God's sheep are being led. You don't simply lead the sheep into new pastures without first knowing anything about it.

Young adults get bored when staying in one place for too long. They have grown up in a world where things are constantly changing, technology is advancing daily. So much so that this generation expects and anticipates new things. That's why whenever Apple comes out with a new iPad or iPhone people stand in lines just to be among the first to have the newest technology. Most of our congregations, on the other hand, find a worship style and way of operating that they like, and they want to stay right there. In the church, we do not want change.

When young adults encounter our change resistance, their relationship with us is short-lived. But consider this for a moment: the young adult culture of upgrade and change is a natural fit for the pastor. Pastors must look for and lead their congregations to the next pasture, where the sheep can be fed and satisfied spiritually. We may find ourselves feeling unstable in this strange and ever-changing culture. But as pastors we should also see the opportunities inherent in this new world, and be inspired. The pastor's task is all about upgrade and change. The trick is to help more seasoned Christians understand that God is always doing a new thing. We will explore ways to accomplish this in a later chapter.

Congregations generally reach those they are intentional about reaching, and for most congregations that is other churchgoers. The church has developed real expertise in reaching people who already belong to a church. Our worship styles, language, and ministries are geared toward already-churched people. New members are often transfers from other congregations rather than people who are actually new to church. We may be successful in adding numbers to our membership rolls, but the Kingdom's membership rolls stay the same.

Contextualize the Message

A common concern about leading congregations to reach young adults is that the gospel must somehow be watered down. But this is not true. Reaching young people is not a matter of changing or watering down the gospel—it is about changing the methods by which we share it. It is an issue for pastors of adapting the message. The culture around us is constantly changing, and adaptive leadership is required in order to reach the young people in it. It has been noted that the congregations to whom the apostles wrote in the first century (Corinth, Thessalonica, Ephesus, etc.) aren't around today. That is not because those congregations did not love Jesus. It is because they did not make the proper adjustments in their ministries to the meet the needs of the changing world. That is why it is so critical that pastors spend time assessing where the congregation is, where it ought to go, and whom it ought to be striving to reach.

46

Adaptive change must be intentional, and it takes effort. But it is possible to adapt our well-worn methods and techniques in order to reach new people in this new age. To understand what this looks like, we might take a lesson from Hollywood.

But it is possible to adapt our well-worn methods and techniques in order to reach new people in this new age.

The story of King Kong was first made into a movie in 1933. The filmmakers used clay animation to create the great ape. In 1976 the classic film was remade, but this time the filmmakers brought the story to life with trick cinematography and a robotic King Kong. King Kong appeared on screen again in 2005. This time, rather than using old methods, the filmmakers created a digital King Kong. This Kong looks much more lifelike than his predecessors.

Each King Kong was created using the technology and tools that were available at the time. Had the 1976 film used clay animation like the original, it would not have done well. Had the 2005 film used the technology of the 1976 film, it would have been a box-office flop. Each filmmaker told the story of King Kong in a way that spoke to that particular generation. The story itself remained the same, but *the way it was told* was new each time.

Sharing the gospel in new ways doesn't mean changing the gospel or watering it down. It does mean that our methods must be different. As pastors, we must understand the people we are aiming to reach. We must determine how they are most likely to be reached. We must adapt our old methods and adopt new ones. My first ministry appointment was a predominately older white congregation in the center of a predominately black neighborhood with young families. By the time I arrived the community already had a negative perception of the congregation, and it was very difficult to shift that perception. The church clung to old models of ministry while the world around it changed drastically. We so often fail to adapt to changing times, hoping (ignorantly) that we will reach twenty-first-century people using twentieth-century methods.

Who Are Our Neighbors?

There is another important aspect to this intentional process of adaptive change: we pastors must know and understand the people in the surrounding community. To know and understand the people around us, we must get out of our churches and meet them, interact with their families, be involved in their community. And this is not a once- or twice-a-year activity; we must authentically and continually be "out there." This is especially true and absolutely critical if the people in the community are not like you.

When I arrived at my first appointment, many of the members took the initiative to inform me that the congregation needed to do something to reach the young people in the neighborhood because the community was changing. It seemed like a strange comment to me because in my estimation, the community was not changing—it had already changed. The question, "What are we going to do to meet the changing needs of the neighborhood?" should have been asked fifteen years earlier.

It is the pastor's role to constantly look at where a congregation needs to go and how to get there. In other words, cast the vision, which is one of the essentials of the pastoral role. Remember, wherever a congregation is in its journey, it cannot stay there. This requires something significant from the congregation as well. The congregants must be open-minded and openhearted. They must see this vision as their priority—not just the pastor's. They must embrace it and embody it. They must allow the pastor to spend time surveying the people in the community, learning about them, and developing relationships with them. The congregants must help the pastor to prioritize the planning, preparation, and equipping necessary to send the congregation out into that community, and to meet the needs of that community. If congregations don't adjust and adapt and allow the pastor to lead toward the vision in these ways, the pastor will be forced to play the role of caretaker. He will slip off the vision track, off the leader track, and onto the dead-end track of manager, keeper of the status quo. We must gently and compassionately—but firmly—require our congregants to think through these issues. We must guide them to consider and discern what is the purpose of their church—Christ's church. We must walk alongside them as they decide to follow our lead into this new vision, and we must hold them accountable to keep putting one foot in front of the other as we carry the gospel into our communities, into the homes and hearts of people who are not like us.

We must gently and compassionately—but firmly—require our congregants to think through these issues.

Other pastors were sent in to make the necessary changes at the church where I had served, but it was too late. Some other congregations in that area were successful in making adjustments. The pastors were able to communicate the vision and to lead their congregations forward. The congregants came to understand the purpose of their churches in new ways, and they allowed their pastors to lead them into this new territory. These churches met the needs of the people in their communities.

Let's examine more closely what it looks like to meet the needs of the people in our changing communities. One critical way to succeed in this area is to be more inclusive.

The Apostle Paul is an excellent example for modern pastors. Paul was never satisfied with simply reaching people in and around his home base of Jerusalem or his hometown of Tarsus. Paul constantly looked for new ways to include new people. Paul wanted to know, "Who needs to receive the gospel, and what do I need to do to make it accessible for them?" Because Paul was well versed in Greek philosophy and Roman culture, he was successful in taking the gospel to new places and helping previously excluded people understand how the good news was for them, too. The Gentiles were unfamiliar with the Hebrew scriptures. They did not speak the Christians' "language." But Paul found ways to include them anyway.

In the same manner, pastors must be willing to lead their congregations into new territory. Failure to go into uncharted territory means that we are ignoring Jesus's mandate. In essence it means pastors (conductors) are leading congregations off the track. Many young adults are like those Gentiles Paul reached out to in the first century. Many young adults have not grown up in a church. For some baby boomers that seems rather odd because they grew up in a time in which going to church was the norm. However, for Generation Xers and millennials, going to church every Sunday was something that many of their peers did not do. So the Christian scriptures and church culture are as strange to them as the gospel message Paul preached to the Gentiles. I remember teaching a Bible study made up of all baby boomers. I asked the group how many people they grew up with did not go to church on a regular basis. The ten group members knew a total of seven people. I shared with them, to their surprise, that I knew dozens. I knew more people who did not grow up in a church than all of them combined.

A Seeker-Friendly Congregation

When we invite into worship young adults who did not grow up in the church—which increasingly is *many* of them—it is like a blind date. Christian scriptures and church culture are strange to most young people today, just as the gospel message was strange to the Gentiles when Paul shared it centuries ago. Our congregations don't appear to know a lot about young adults, and young adults don't know a lot about the church. We use words they are not familiar with, such as *narthex, doxology, Communion,* and *sanctification.* United Methodists use acronyms that mean nothing to our guests, such as UMM, VBS, UMW, UMYF, and GBOD. We assume that our listeners know this strange language, our customs, and the stories from our scriptures.

Our congregations don't appear to know a lot about young adults, and young adults don't know a lot about the church.

Paul would have had to deal with the same thing. He shared the gospel with people who were unfamiliar with Hebrew prophecy and scriptures. That's why Paul didn't preach to Gentiles as if they knew the Hebrew story. He used language and imagery that spoke to the particular context of the people he was trying to reach. Paul actually taught using reason and philosophy so that his audience could more easily understand and relate to his message. What pastors can learn from this is that Paul was prepared to take the gospel to foreign lands. That is to say, Paul was looking ahead to where the church was being called to go, rather than looking for ways to guard and maintain its current state.

It is important to know that whether a pastor is leading a congregation to reach young adults, start a new ministry for the community, or begin a new worship experience, it is risky. Whenever you venture into uncharted territory, there are risks involved. You risk people giving less because they don't like change. There is the risk that some (or most) of what you try will not work, making it even harder to introduce the next new idea. There is also the risk that people will leave the church when they don't particularly care for the new vision into which you are leading them. Pastoring on track is risky business.

A Long Tradition of Taking Risks

It is also important to know that the Judeo-Christian tradition has come this far because men and women of God, for thousands of years, have been willing to take risks. The father and mother of our faith, Abraham and Sarah, risked everything by leaving the comfort of their homeland to go to a strange new place that God had promised to them. Had they not been willing to take the risk, our story of faith would be completely different. In the same manner Rahab, who lived in Jericho, risked imprisonment and even death by betraying her own people in order to help the Israelites in occupying the city of Jericho. If Rahab had been afraid, the people of God may well have had to hold up on moving into a new territory. There were other Old Testament risk-takers, like Joshua, who was used by God to bring down the walls of Jericho without a single weapon. Gideon challenged the huge and mighty Midianite army with only three hundred soldiers. Don't forget about Queen Esther, who put her personal interests aside in order to save the Israelite people in Babylonian exile. These are just a few of the people in the biblical story who were not afraid to take a risk, a leap of faith to accomplish a greater purpose for God.

The apostles Peter and John were thrown into a Jerusalem jail for preaching the good news of Jesus Christ (Acts 4). The next day they were told by the Sanhedrin to discontinue their preaching. Peter and John had a choice to make. They could follow the instructions and warning given to them by the very people responsible for the death of Jesus, their teacher and friend. Or they could risk ridicule, torture, and death in order to take the gospel to new people. We all know they took the risk, and as a result the church has grown beyond anything they could have possibly imagined. We see the same type of risky behavior from Philip, who was willing to leave Jerusalem after the stoning of Stephen and go to Samaria, a place that was not all that welcoming of Jews. As a result of Philip's courage to venture out beyond Jerusalem, Christianity grew in Samaria.

The church of Jesus Christ has grown from just 120 believers (Acts 1) to over a billion worldwide today because of apostles, teachers, evangelists, bishops, and other clergy who were willing to risk their own safety for the sake of leading the church into new pastures. In fact, it seems that throughout church history those individuals who took the greatest risks made the biggest impact on the church. They appear to have altered the course of church history and brought Christianity into a new era. We are the recipients of the results of their innovation and courage. If the church is going to continue to survive, pastors must carry the mantle that dates back to the time of Abraham and Sarah. We must take risks in order to advance our congregations into a new era of ministry.

One such leader was the German Reformer Martin Luther. This scholar, who did not come from the aristocracy of Germany, stood up to perhaps the most powerful entity in the world at that time, the Roman Catholic Church. Luther saw that the Catholic church was stuck in some practices that he believed went against scripture. He could have easily ignored the problem and continued teaching theology without stirring up trouble. His life would have been a lot easier. However, Martin Luther could not sit idle while the Catholic church dug itself into an immoral hole by selling indulgences. So he challenged the practices of the Catholic church and he was soon after excommunicated. Martin Luther did not intend to start a movement. But a movement rose up around him because he was willing to take a risk. The church universal grew as a result of his behavior. Millions of people today know Christ through the Protestant branch of Christianity because Martin Luther took a risk.

Pastors can learn a lot from Martin Luther about leading

congregations. Many of us have been a part of congregations that have practices or traditions that, although not immoral, are not conducive to vital worship or effective ministry. Often we are too afraid to say or do anything about it because of the consequences that come with challenging such practices that are sacred to the congregations we serve. However, if pastors are really going to be the shepherds that God calls them to be, they will sometimes be required to challenge the status quo and practices that hinder numerical and spiritual growth in a congregation. Standing up to the people who believe those hindering practices and other roadblocks are sacred should be done carefully and compassionately, but it should be done. It is a risk worth taking. It is a risk that comes with the territory of being a pastor.

John Wesley, founder of the Methodist movement, was another instructive risk-taker. Although Wesley remained a member of the Anglican church until the day he died, he started a movement that eventually led to the many different Methodist denominations today. John Wesley appreciated many things in the Anglican church, but he felt the church was not reaching the working-class people of England, the very people they needed to reach. It was his observation that the Anglican church catered more to the middle class, which did not sit well with Wesley. So he began preaching beyond the local parish and taking the gospel to the people. John Wesley crossed parish boundaries in order to preach in fields to those whom the church was not reaching. This caused tension between him and many Anglican leaders. He faced ridicule and sometimes violence in order to reach new people for Christ Jesus. Furthermore, he had a desire to help people establish a deeper relationship with Jesus. He believed there was more to salvation than being saved from the wages of sin. Wesley's forward thinking sparked a holiness movement that resulted in millions of new people coming to know Jesus and continues to expand today.

John Wesley's example reveals to us what pastoral ministry is all about. As we "drive the train," we are called to look for and see the people standing at the side of the tracks in neighborhoods and communities all across our country. I'm talking about those who have grown weary of the church and those who have never had any kind of relationship with Jesus and his church. As pastors we are to lead our congregations into these new territories, to invite new people on board. That's risky because it will certainly mean reaching out to people who are not like us, not like the people already on the train. These newcomers might have a different level of education, socioeconomic background, nationality, or race. Members might question what the pastor is doing and question whether or not these new people will fit in with the old. In spite of those questions and risks, pastors must press forward to lead their congregations to reach new people, keeping in mind that we are where we are today as a church because so many before us were willing to take a risk.

As pastors we are to lead our congregations into these new territories, to invite new people on board.

Charles Harrison Mason was another Christian revolutionary risk-taker. Mason grew up in the Baptist tradition of the church but was eventually led by God to start a new denomination. Mason embraced the new Pentecostal movement that began to spread in the late nineteenth and early twentieth centuries from the teaching of people like Charles Parham and William Seymour. When C. H. Mason accepted speaking in tongues and the Pentecostal message of miracles, healing, and other gifts of the Spirit, he was rejected by ministry partners and congregations. Yet that did not discourage Mason from holding on to his new convictions and eventually reorganizing the Church of God in Christ and becoming its first general overseer.

Mason's story illustrates another important aspect of pastoral leadership and the essential function of leading into new territory. As pastors, we must lead into new places not only because that is where we will reach and include new people but also because God will then be revealed in new ways. We, and our congregants, will understand and relate to God more deeply or in ways that are more meaningful. The kingdom of God is creative and dynamic, and when we lead people into new ways of experiencing that Kingdom, we are opening new ways for the Kingdom to expand. Charles Mason took a risk in preaching and teaching something that was not common among his peers and friends in the Baptist tradition. His risk resulted in a worldwide movement that spawned other Pentecostal denominations such as the Assemblies of God in Christ and the Pentecostal Assemblies of the World.

How many new ministries, new congregations, and new converts does the church miss out on because pastors are not willing to risk preaching a new concept to their congregations? To risk teaching something different such as a new understanding of who and what a pastor is called to be? To risk teaching new concepts such as the validity of speaking in tongues, new spiritual disciplines such as fasting or silence, new musical experiences in worship, or new emphasis in ministry, such as service in mission to the poor? Conflict may arise when we teach these new concepts. People will often reject new ideas, because they are different from what they've always thought and experienced. We are all fearful of the unfamiliar. Yet, without pastors taking those risks of teaching boldly and without fear as C. H. Mason did, congregations will miss out on new food to satisfy the soul. It is essential that we pastors lead into new territory, or our congregations will slow to a crawl, spinning in place on the track, and eventually completely stall out.

Congregations will never enter new territory unless the pastor and congregational leaders are risk-takers. There are people outside of our faith communities who are looking for meaning and purpose in life. When we as pastors are not willing to deal with people and obstacles, we are in effect choosing to leave the bystanders at the station house, on the side of the track, left out and excluded from the gospel meant for all.

Questions for Reflection

1. What is the biggest risk your congregation has ever taken?

2. What is the biggest risk you've taken in your personal faith journey?

3. Why is there so much talk about the church reaching younger generations and not older generations?

4. How can the church reach out to younger generations without ignoring older generations?

Chapter 5

Essential: Develop Leaders around the Vision

Then he said to them, "Therefore, every legal expert who has been trained as a disciple for the kingdom of heaven is like the head of a household who brings old and new things out of their treasure chest."
—Matthew 13:52

I realize that it's easy for me to write a book and say that a pastor should focus on leading the congregation. Some of you will perhaps read this and say that it's easier said than done. After all, we have structures and boards in place in our congregations that can cause problems when it comes to the pastor-as-leader model. For many, the denominational polity will not allow you to just change the structure within a local congregation. My rebuttal is that you don't have to change the structure as much as you have to change your and others' mind-sets.

In order for congregations to effectively make disciples for Jesus Christ, everyone must understand their role. Unfortunately, many church boards get in the wrong lane and try to take on the God-given role of the pastor. It is the pastor's role, according to scripture, to serve as the visionary for the church. The pastor is the spiritual leader and must have the freedom to lead. The church board's role should be to support the pastor's vision and establish policies so that the vision can flourish.

59

The church board's role should be to support the pastor's vision and establish policies so that the vision can flourish.

God gives the vision for a congregation to the pastor, and the board has the task of helping the pastor carry out that vision. Some might argue that it is the pastor along with the board, deacons, and elders who set the vision of the church. It's not that other leaders don't help with the vision, because they do. But please remember that pastor means "shepherd," and Psalm 23 suggests that it is the pastor who leads the sheep to green pastures.

Let's look at this from a practical perspective. If the pastor has to share the visioning with other church leaders, there are bound to be disagreements. This then leads to stalemates. Which direction do we go? Whose plan should we follow? Congregations often experience decline and conflict because the pastor's vision is different from the leadership board's vision. The only thing this does is prevent the congregation from growing and effectively making disciples for Jesus Christ.

To take this a step further, if the pastor's job is to simply follow the vision laid out by the church's leadership board, how can he or she effectively preach and teach the word of God? To follow the lead of a board would mean that the pastor must teach based on a vision that God did not give him or her. To me this concept seems awkward, unappealing, and a hindrance for the preaching ministry. It would almost be like the movie *Chocolat*, where in a small Italian town the mayor controlled everything including the local church. Before the pastor preached every Sunday morning, the mayor had to review his sermon to make sure that it lined up with his beliefs and vision. This might be the extreme, but I think you get the point. Although a church board may not review the sermon prior to the pastor preaching it, it is just as stifling to have the board set the vision that the pastor has to follow. The model would suggest that the congregation doesn't need a pastor but someone who can follow directions.

It is extremely difficult to accomplish a lot when there has to be a vote on every decision. Things come up in the life of a church constantly, and if a pastor has to get the approval of the board to do most things, not much will get done. Very few, if any, effective organizations operate without one person calling the shots on the day-to-day operations. The reason it takes so long to accomplish things at times is precisely because many pastors must receive the permission of a board. If pastors were routinely granted the authority (although the Bible gives the pastor this authority, it is not the case in many congregational structures) to set the vision and to have their teams carry it out, you would see more congregations bursting with vitality.

I realize that for many congregations, allowing the pastor to set the vision may be strange and difficult. In several congregations this is a shared responsibility. Furthermore, what if the congregants don't like the direction the pastor is taking them? What if they disagree with where they are going? Well, just think you will not be alone. When Moses led the people out of Egypt, they complained about every step of the way. Just imagine what would have happened if the elders of all the tribes had gathered and told Moses that they should have a vote in deciding where the people went. It would have been pure chaos. They would have probably never been able to cross the Red Sea because the board would have said no.

The reality of the matter is that God gave the vision to Moses to lead the people. The people would either get on board or be left behind. Likewise, today God gives the vision to the pastor to lead the congregation. Since God did not give the vision to the elders of Israel they could either trust that Moses really was appointed by God or not. I'm not suggesting that the board and congregation should blindly follow the pastor's lead. The pastor should and must be open to questions, suggestions, and perhaps even help in framing the vision. One way to accomplish this is for the pastor to gather

61

the leaders and lead them through the visioning process. This allows laity to be involved in the visioning under the guidance of the pastor. I believe it is important for the leadership of the church to help develop and outline the vision. No congregation should follow without first having clarity. This means that the pastor, just like a shepherd, persuades the sheep to move and must cast the vision so that people can catch it, embrace it, and follow.

It is important for the leadership of the church to help develop and outline the vision. No congregation should follow without first having clarity.

The pastor must be able to articulate the where and the why of the vision. Even Moses had to first explain those two things before the people would follow. Moses explained why: so they could worship God freely. Moses explained where: to the land God had promised to Abraham, Isaac, and Jacob. Moses also had to get approval from the elders. I would assume those elders asked plenty of questions, gave some suggestions, and even helped Moses frame the vision. So before they left Egypt the vision was clear; even though there were hiccups along the way, the people knew where they were going. Furthermore, the people followed Moses because they knew he was called, anointed, and appointed by God. This leads to the most important reason why a congregation should follow the lead of the pastor. It is because he or she has been called and set aside by God to lead. If a congregation does not believe that their pastor is called by God, that is a problem. However, if you believe that your pastor is called, anointed, and appointed by God, then give the pastor the freedom to do exactly what God called him or her to do—lead.

John Edmund Kaiser, in his book, *Winning on Purpose*,[1] does a great job of explaining how a congregation ought to operate. The pastor leads and the church board governs and the disciples within the congregation do ministry. That board governs by establishing and maintaining the policies and procedures that dictate how the church operates. This does not mean the board manages the day-to-day operations but rather simply oversees them. The board lays out the policies and enforces them.

The best example of this can be found in the fifteenth chapter of the book of Acts, which describes a time when issues arose out of the congregations in Antioch, Syria, and Cilicia. These Gentiles had recently converted to the faith, and there were questions about some of their pagan practices. There were also questions as to whether or not these Gentiles should be circumcised, as was the Jewish custom. Paul and Silas even had a heated discussion about what would be acceptable. They could not come to a conclusion on the matter, so they took it to the apostles and the elders, the council or what we would call the church governing board. After much discussion, these church leaders came to the conclusion that some of those Gentile practices did not violate Christian values. The council laid out the policy that they could not eat food sacrificed to idols or food with blood still in it, and they had to abstain from sexual immorality. Notice that the council only put together the policy. They did not tell those congregations how to execute it or how to share it with the members. It was up to Paul and Silas to implement it, and the leaders of those congregations would carry it out. They set the policy so that the pastors of those congregations could lead. Furthermore, you notice that the council or church board did not take an official vote. Apparently they came to a common understanding. How great would it be if our church leadership boards would set policies by coming to a common agreement of what is best for the church?

The day-to-day management of the church does not fall on the pastor but on the pastor's team. In a large church this generally means paid staff: a person to oversee the operations, a person to manage the ministries, and a person to manage the weekly worship experience. For the smaller congregation, this might mean the pastor appoints trusted men and women to handle these things. In either case, the team will need to meet with the pastor on a regular basis in order to carry out the vision within the guidelines established by the board.

There are at least two reasons why the operations of the church should be handled by individuals rather than the board. First, when you manage things by committee, it's harder to get consensus. The members might disagree on where and how to handle things. Things move a lot slower this way. I've heard many people say, and I have experienced it myself, how slow things move in the church. This is true because in many congregations you have to get a committee on board with an idea and then it has to go on to the next committee before anything can happen. This is problematic because there is something always going on in a church. Ministry is thwarted when things are at a standstill because of disagreement.

Second, when the pastor has a vision it's harder to carry that vision out if first it must be taken to a large body rather than a small trusted team. When it is time to move the congregation, the pastor ought to be able to go to his or her management team to get them on board. They in turn get their teams on board and the vision begins to spread. This also creates a direct line of accountability. Everyone knows whom to go to with their questions. Team leaders understand and embrace the vision, as do staff leaders, committee chairs, and those closest to the pastor. The vision and the plans to move toward the vision are passed from leader to leader, throughout the church leadership structure. Individual team leaders, armed with this understanding and the marching orders, can make decisions quickly for their particular ministry areas and can move the congregation to where the pastor is leading.

Individual team leaders, armed with this understanding and the

marching orders, can make decisions quickly for their particular ministry areas and can move the congregation to where the pastor is leading.

When Moses put his team together after his father-in-law urged him to do so, the team members managed everything under the vision of Moses. This allowed Moses to focus on the larger picture. Notice that they did not use committees to manage the affairs of the people but rather leaders, who were held accountable and who understood Moses's vision. When Moses utilized this model things ran a lot more smoothly. That's why it's better to have trusted people who have been empowered to manage daily operations within the parameters set by the board. The pastor of the church must be empowered to set the vision and to lead in the way God intends. This sometimes means changing things around, even the budget, in order to meet the goal.

The members of the congregation, as Kaiser explains, are then freed up to be actively engaged in ministry. This, of course, means members need to know how and where to get involved. If the pastor is the leader, how do members understand their roles? How do they see where they fit into the plans? One important way is through the individual's discovery of personal spiritual gifts. Just like the pastor has gifts for ministry, so too does each member of the body of Christ.

Not only is it important for there to be a team in place to govern the church, but also I want to stress the importance of policies and procedures. If the pastor is to be truly freed up to shepherd the people, there must be clear guiding principles in place. Otherwise, the pastor might easily find himself or herself in the position of making decisions on issues that arise each week. I remember when the church I pastor first transitioned to a model that had a governing board to oversee the larger picture as it related to personnel, finances, and property. However, we lacked operational policies and procedures for some of the everyday occurrences.

For example, we often have outside community groups that want to use space in our building. A representative from a group might call and request to speak to the pastor and ask if they could use our facilities. Or they would ask one of our administrators to ask the pastor. I would then be left with the task of having to decide if it was appropriate for them to use the building based on time, date, number of people, and so on. The problem was that the task required time and energy that could have been spent in study, prayer, writing, or planning. I guess it would have been fine if it was something that happened periodically, but it seemed that I was making decisions on things like that three or four times a week.

The best way to handle these issues so that the pastor can focus on pastoral matters is to develop an operational manual with forms, vouchers, and guidelines. An operational manual frees the pastor and even other leaders from spending their time making decisions because people then have something in writing to refer to. The manual spells out how, when, where, and what things can be done in and for the church without taking time away from a pastor's true obligations. Remember, if a pastor is exerting his or her energy governing or managing, that means he or she is not fulfilling the biblical job description.

An operational manual frees the pastor and even other leaders from spending their time making decisions because people then have something in writing to refer to.

Questions for Reflection

1. Can you think of some ways in the past where ministry in your congregation was stifled because too many committees were involved?

2. How is the vision set at your church?

3. What might be some challenges in allowing the pastor to set the vision?

4. What are ways church leaders can help a pastor set the vision for the church?

Chapter 6

Essential: Teach and Preach

But he said to them, "I must preach the good news of God's kingdom in other cities too, for this is why I was sent."

—*Luke 4:43*

The Pastor's Job Description

I remember when I was a seminary student in Ohio and eager to get started in ministry. In those days I would go from church to church on Sundays just to see what established pastors were doing and to hear good preaching. One Sunday I visited one of the largest congregations in Columbus, Ohio. The hospitality was fantastic, the choir was anointed, and then came the preacher. The pastor's message was theologically sound and practical, but there was one statement in the sermon that blew my mind. He told the congregation, "If you all handle the business of the church and take care of the ministry, I promise I will feed you." What I understood him to mean was that he would feed them with the word of God through preaching and teaching if he did not have to get bogged down with other things like a bunch of meetings and church management.

This was strange to me because it seemed to go against everything

69

I had heard and seen when it came to vocational ministry. I always understood the pastor's role to be that of teacher/preacher but also lead administrator. It was my contention, at least at that time, that the pastor should be involved in the day-to-day operations of the church. So how could a pastor of such a prominent church say that he wanted only to teach, preach, and lead the congregation?

It took me several years of pastoral ministry before I finally came to understand exactly what that pastor meant. I was sitting at home one evening looking at our church budget as I was preparing for our finance meeting the next day. Then I began to think about the trustee meeting, the church council meeting, and all the other meetings I had to attend. I began to wonder why I had gone to seminary in the first place. As I stated in a previous chapter, I have often heard other pastors say they wished they'd had additional training so they would have been more prepared to manage their churches. I used to try to count how many hours each week I spent studying and teaching compared to how many hours I spent on administration. It wasn't too long before I understood what that Columbus pastor meant. It slowly dawned on me that I had come to agree with him. That realization led me to begin a real study of what the Bible actually says about the role of the pastor.

The Conductor

The pastor's role, using our train metaphor, is analogous to that of the conductor. As already mentioned, it's important to remember that metaphors break down eventually. But at the least an examination of the word *conductor* is interesting and instructive. It is most fascinating even beyond the train conductor, revealing more about the job description of pastor. Let's take a closer look at five aspects of the definition of the word *conductor*. According to *Dictionary.com*, a conductor is:

1. "a leader, guide, director, or manager";

2. a person "on a bus, train, or other public conveyance, who is

in charge of the conveyance and its passengers," the people on board;

3. a person who communicates his interpretation of a musical score or other written work to performers;

4. a "body... that readily conducts heat, electricity, sound, etc."; and

5. a "lightning rod."[1]

The first two aspects relate to the conductor in our train metaphor: as pastors we are to lead, guide and direct. We are to be "in charge," that is, to use the authority with which we have been ordained. This means that we must be strong and confident enough to make difficult and sometimes unpopular decisions on behalf of our "charge."

We must be strong and confident enough to make difficult and sometimes unpopular decisions on behalf of our "charge."

But the further meanings of the word are also instructive: We are to interpret and communicate the "music" of God's word in scripture, to express it in such a way that others can join in that expression, so that even those who are passively listening or observing may hear and understand. We are to conduct the grace, mercy, and love of God through the power of the Holy Spirit and to share that power with others, thus empowering them to do the same. Finally, we are lightning rods! As we lead and move our churches toward new visions, we must absorb the inevitable shocks of negative feedback, from outside the congregation and from within it. We must be able to take the heat.

The Shepherd: Feeding the Sheep

Turning to scripture, we learn still more about a pastor's job description, particularly in the example of the shepherd. The job of the shepherd was to protect the sheep from predators and to ensure that they had food to eat. That's why in John 21, before Jesus ascended to heaven, Jesus told Peter to feed his sheep. Jesus was referring not to physical food but to spiritual food. Jesus wanted to make sure that his apostles would feed the people the word of God and share his teachings with the world. It was so important to Jesus and so vital to the Kingdom movement he had started that he gave this directive to Peter three times. Today, the responsibility falls on shepherds/pastors to make sure Jesus's lambs are fed often and fed properly.

Again, this was why the office of deacon was established. The apostles wanted to make sure those given the task of teaching could spend the proper time preparing and delivering. It's not just deacons who take some of the load off the pastor but also other leaders, associate pastors, staff, and key volunteers. All areas of ministry and operations are important in the life of a congregation. No area can be left untended. When all areas of the church are covered, then the pastor can truly focus on feeding Jesus's sheep.

In order for the sheep that belong to Jesus to be fed as well as those who do not yet belong to him, the shepherds must remain focused on preparing the food. I use the metaphor of preparing the food to suggest that prayer and study should consume a great deal of a pastor's week. The primary role of the pastor is to teach and preach the word of God. The only way that pastors can present the word in fresh, practical, and relevant ways is to move away from the management business and get into the habit of spending a significant and consistent amount of time each week praying, studying, writing, and preparing. For me, that amounts to thirty hours or more weekly.

One might view the pastor's time in study and payer as preparing the food to feed the sheep so that the pastor can do what is required of her or him. Paul puts the requirements this way: "[Christ] gave some apostles, some prophets, some evangelists, and some pastors and teachers. His purpose was to equip God's people for the work of serving and building up the body of Christ until we all reach the unity of faith and knowledge of God's Son. God's goal is for us to become mature adults—to be fully grown, measured by the standard of the fullness of Christ" (Ephesians 4:11-13). Equipping or feeding the sheep is the primary responsibility of the pastor. It's interesting that Paul does not write about the pastor doing other ministry; rather, the saints (the congregation) are the ones engaged in reaching, touching, and serving people for the sake of the gospel. One could easily ask the question: Does this mean the pastor is not involved in ministry? Quite the contrary; equipping the saints is the ministry of the pastor. That is what we have been trained to do. So the ministry of any local congregation begins with the ministry of the pastor feeding the sheep so that they can be actively engaged in ministry.

Seminary education prepares pastors to think theologically and to understand the gospel message for today. Receiving a master's of divinity or master's in theological studies or even training at a Bible college is not the equivalent of receiving a master's of business administration with an emphasis in Bible. Pastors are not trained business administrators; we are trained practical theologians who have been forced to become administrators in our congregations (some better than others because they have the gift of administration). The first time I actually dealt with a budget on an organizational level was at my first church council meeting right out of seminary. It was new to me, and I thought to myself, "I don't remember taking this class in seminary." Although some seminaries may offer more classes today on finances and administration, I believe this is moving us away from what God called pastors to do—to feed Jesus's sheep.

73

The Shepherd: Appointing Others

Feeding God's people was such a serious matter that the first part of Acts 6 deals with its importance. As the church began to grow, the teaching responsibilities of the apostles grew. In addition, the needs of the church also grew. There were more and more people in need of special attention. That's when some of the Greek-influenced Jews began to question some of the non-Greek-influenced Jews. The Hellenistic Jews were concerned that their widows were not being served food in the same manner as the Hebraic Jews. The matter came before the apostles because there needed to be a fair resolution. How the apostles handled the situation could have thwarted or enhanced the Jesus movement.

Rather than try to divide the work of serving the widows among the twelve apostles, they came up with a better solution. Acts 6:3 tells us they decided to appoint and anoint seven men to serve as deacons who would have the responsibility of serving the widows. The reason behind this newly created office in the church was so that the apostles would not neglect what Jesus had charged them to do. Jesus wanted them to feed the sheep on a spiritual level, not just on a physical or emotional level. This is not to say that there wasn't a concern for the widows, because the apostles cared deeply about their physical and emotional needs. That's why they were very careful in the selection process for the seven deacons.

It is important to note that the apostles did not take on the job themselves, because their work was much broader. It was not geared specifically toward one group but toward the entire church as a whole. Furthermore, they had to direct a great deal of their attention toward people who were not a part of the church. In order to do that effectively, they had to delegate some of the administrative and service responsibilities to others. Delegation can be a challenge to many pastors today because the people they serve want to hear or see the pastor, especially when they are sick and in the hospital. There is no question that visiting the sick is a critical part of church ministry. However, the pastor has many responsibilities in addition to visitation. Sometimes visitations can be done by the pastor, but at other times others who have spiritual gifts to suit that ministry will have to fill that role. That is something we will discuss a little later. It really all depends on the week and what's going on and especially the size of the congregation. Keep in mind that the pastor may not be able to visit everyone, but the pastor can provide care for all members by way of feeding the congregation, who in turn feed those in need.

The Shepherd: Letting Go

> Not only does chapter 6 of Acts show pastors what ought to be the primary focus of ministry, but it also shows that pastors don't have to do everything.

The apostles' teaching and preaching responsibilities were so critical for the success of the movement that they had to let some other things go. Things they did when the church was smaller they could no longer do. Not only does chapter 6 of Acts show pastors what ought to be the primary focus of ministry, but it also shows that pastors don't have to do everything. Instead of declaring they would take care of the widows *and* proclaim the word of God, they appointed other disciples to use their gifts, spreading the responsibilities across the growing body of Christ. That's a challenge to many pastors who have a need to be involved in every aspect of ministry. The pastor's involvement centers on teaching what and how Christians should treat one another based on God's word. Great ministry doesn't take place without first teaching what Christian ministry is and its purpose. Pastors should be aware of and should understand what is happening in the ministries of the church. We are the conductors—directing, guiding, and "in charge," and so we must be knowledgeable. But that does not mean we are to be directly *doing* the work, making day-to-day decisions, and involved in the many details of the ministries. Our job is to feed the people—to interpret and communicate God's word, to teach and preach, so that effective ministry can and will take place.

Our job is to feed the people—to conduct the power of the Holy Spirit, to interpret and communicate God's word, to teach and preach, so that effective ministry can and will take place.

The Spiritual Gifts

The spiritual food that God's sheep receive from the pastor enables the sheep to carry out their tasks as members of the body of Christ. Each member has a responsibility or an assignment. Each member's assignment is based upon his or her spiritual gifts. The gifts of the Spirit are the very characteristics of God manifested in the person of Jesus of Nazareth. Jesus invites his disciples to participate in Kingdom activity. In order for us to accomplish this daunting task, the Holy Spirit, as promised, is freely given to enable believers to live in the power and presence of Jesus. Believers, through the power of the Spirit, are extensions of Jesus's ministry. Spiritual gifts are the mark that one has been filled with the Spirit and living in Christ.

It is vital for each community of faith to know that no one person contains all of Jesus's attributes but that everyone has some characteristic that allows God's grace to shine in and through them. All believers are endowed with gifts; it's not something for a select few. Collectively we make up the body of Christ, and each individual has a different function or ministry based on his or her gifts. Spiritual gifts are more than tools given by God to ensure the success of the ministries of the church; they are the lifeblood of the church and what it represents. In other words, we can't be the church of Jesus Christ without the gifts of the Spirit. We would merely be an organization that tries to do nice things for people.

> # Spiritual gifts are more than tools given by God to ensure the success of the ministries of the church; they are the lifeblood of the church and what it represents.

When the Apostle Paul talks about equipping the saints, he is referring to teaching believers to know who they are in Christ Jesus. The equipping occurs primarily through preaching, teaching, and casting the vision. Pastors, we must order our weeks so that we may devote ourselves to study, prayer, writing, and preparation to serve as effective conductors and to feed God's sheep. Let us turn now to a more in-depth discussion of that task.

The Pastor as Teacher and Preacher

Feeding the lambs that belong to Jesus is accomplished in many different ways. We have Bible studies and training events where a portion of our congregations participate and are fed. We feed people one-on-one in pastoral counseling sessions and by ministering to members through visitations. I've often said it does not matter how much we advertise, and no matter how good our Bible studies and training events are, they still don't reach as many people as are fed in our worship experiences each week. Worship, not Bible studies or training events, is the largest venue in which the pastor is able to cast the vision; provide pastoral care, marriage counseling, and family counseling; offer spiritual formation; and deploy people for service into the community. The preaching moment is when the pastor is able to feed the most people at one time. It is the place where new ministries can be launched, the time in which care is given and the future of the church is spelled out to the congregation as a whole. When I began the doctor of ministry program at Saint Paul School of Theology, I wanted to focus on spiritual formation, and it was Pastor Zan Holmes (pastor emeritus) who gave me some sound advice. He told me that whatever my focus was for the doctoral program, I should be sure to incorporate preaching into my studies. He declared that just about everything he started during his pastorate at St. Luke's Community United Methodist Church in Dallas was introduced during a sermon. Pastor Holmes told me that preaching is the springboard from which new initiatives and ministries are launched.

> The preaching moment is when the pastor is able to feed the most people at one time. It is the place where new ministries can be launched, the time in which care is given and the future of the church is spelled out to the congregation as a whole.

It is for all of these reasons that pastors ought to take very seriously the preaching ministry. It is much more than just another duty of a pastor. The only time many people receive spiritual nourishment is on Sunday morning when they listen to the preacher preach.

Several years ago I took my children to a petting zoo. We got there right before feeding time. I remember one of the workers came in to feed the animals, and as she entered the area with the food, all the animals rushed to get close to her. She began reaching into the bucket and spreading the food around and the animals just ate. They ate until she was completely out of food. She dusted her hands off as she left the area, and almost as if it were rehearsed, the animals went back to what they were doing before she came in with the food. I imagine the preaching moment happening in similar fashion. Each week the sheep that belong to Jesus gather in the house of the Lord to be fed. They all look to the pastor to provide them with food, and when it is over they leave the sanctuary and go back to their normal lives. If the preaching does not properly satisfy them, they will not have the strength to handle the ups and downs that life throws at them during the week. I've been taught that I ought to prepare and deliver a sermon each week as if someone's life depends on it, because we truly never know when that might be the case. If pastors are going to effectively lead congregations, there must be an understanding, appreciation, and reverence given to the primary vehicle for feeding people, which is preaching.

In worship celebrations all over the world pastors stand before congregations to preach. In many churches preaching is the climax of the worship experience, the moment of anticipation and expectation: expecting to hear what God has to say about their lives and anticipating nourishment of their souls. Although preaching can be defined simply as giving a message about God, there are many aspects of preaching that are not as easily defined. Before we can understand what it means to preach, we must first explore the principles of preaching. Having a proper comprehension of what it means to preach and what purpose it serves is a good place to begin understanding the concept of feeding Jesus' lambs. What we cannot forget when feeding/preaching is the intended audience of the preacher and by whose authority the preaching occurs. The content and form of a sermon are vital aspects in the makeup of preaching. What makes an action preaching as opposed to delivering a lecture or a speech depends on the preacher's perception of the word of God. This is the most important aspect of preaching because it holds all the other principles together. All of these principles play a critical role in the process of providing spiritual food for the people.

One thing that distinguishes preaching from giving a speech is the act of proclaiming. Christian preaching is the proclamation throughout the globe of God's saving activity, through Christ Jesus, working in the world and how we might gain access to that power. The proclamation or kerygmatic aspect of preaching deals with the announcement of the good news. That announcement is not just of the teachings of the church. It also involves the uncompromising beliefs of the preacher. One cannot pronounce something boldly and with passion if he or she is uncertain whether or not it is true. The pastor is charged with demanding that the listener turn away from his or her former self and accept a new life and lifestyle through Jesus. Pastors are to proclaim Jesus Christ's redeeming love unapologetically and with holy boldness. The act of proclaiming implies confidence and certainty. The message is intended to inspire others to become more faithful servants of God. That's why pastors feed the sheep, so that people are drawn closer to and more committed to God. It is important that pastors declare the good news in such a way that the proclamation is the courageous certainty, manifested throughout the sermon, and that the bold announcement taking place is truth.

Not only does feeding God's sheep involve proclamation, but it should also entail an instructional component (*didache*). How can one live out the good news and go where God's shepherd is leading if one is unaware of how to apply the good news to daily life? As I listen to several preachers, it is evident today that not all preaching involves teaching; however, I believe preaching is the primary tool within the church for shaping and forming the community of believers. While proclamation (*kerygma*) deals with the act and the subject of preaching, teaching (*didache*) expresses the how of preaching. If we have established that the saving power of Jesus is that which is proclaimed, the next question becomes, "How is that relevant in my daily life?" It is my contention that preaching ought to contain some teaching that instructs believers in how to live out the good news of Jesus once they have accepted God's offer of salvation through Christ.

The teachings from the apostles in the first century dealt with instructions for worship, directions for church leaders, and the ways of death and life.[2] The apostles understood that in order for believers to live like believers, they needed to receive food that instructed them on how to live. If the church is to carry on its tradition of Christian living, then pastors' preaching must include not only a bold announcement of who Jesus Christ is but also directions and instructions for believers to carry out. When it comes to preaching, the teaching component should be concerned with what the hearers do once the act of preaching is concluded. In other words, preaching ought to leave each hearer of the word with something that informs them of how to live out a Christian life. If preaching declares that God's love for humanity is evident in Jesus, the preaching also ought to include instruction on how to respond to that love through our actions. Simply put, the preaching ought to be fulfilled in the lives of the believers. That's what Jesus shared in his first public sermon (Luke 4). Those who were there in that synagogue heard the message and they then were able to watch that message lived out in Jesus.

I believe the proclaiming (*kerygmatic*) aspect of preaching inspires and transforms one to become a faithful servant of God. However, the teaching (*didactic*) aspect of preaching educates the hearer on how to live out that inspiration. One thing that the teaching of Jesus instructed believers to do was to go out and make more disciples. According to Matthew 28:16-20, this was the last instruction Jesus left his church before he ascended to the right hand of the Father.

The fact that the Great Commission was the last thing taught to the disciples of Jesus confirms its importance. This means the hearers of the word should be transformed in such a way that they are inspired to preach to nonbelievers. So in essence, one result of the teaching aspect of preaching should be to lead hearers to participate in the proclamation of the church. Pastors are to spiritually feed parishioners so they can feed the world.

The proclaiming (*kerygmatic*) aspect of preaching inspires one to become a faithful servant of God. The teaching (*didactic*) aspect of preaching educates the hearer on how to live out that inspiration.

Now that we have established what and how a pastor ought to feed Jesus's sheep through preaching, it is time to define who the pastor is as preacher. The simple definition of a Christian preacher is one who proclaims the gospel; he or she is the message giver. It is the preacher's job to convey the message of hope, victory, liberation, and deliverance through Jesus Christ. Pastors must be in tune with a variety of things, including the Bible, social issues, congregational dynamics, and the needs of the community. Preaching professor Thomas Long puts it this way: "Preaching requires such gifts as a sensitivity to human need, a discerning eye for the connections between faith and life, an ear attuned to hearing the voice of scripture, compassion, a growing personal faith, and the courage to tell the truth."[3]

Although it is the preacher who is delivering the good news message, it is actually God who is speaking through the preacher.[4] Each individual preacher has a role to play in the preaching moment in that she or he must be faithful in preparation. Just as any good chef takes time in preparing exquisite food (it doesn't happen by accident), so too a pastor must be intentional in preparing a sermon, meaning the pastor must put forth the effort to study, pray, and meditate over scripture in order to hear from God. When a pastor is faithful in preparation, the Holy Spirit will aid that pastor to bring the sermon to life. It is as though God is saying to pastors, "If you put forth effort to prepare a sermon, I will not simply match your effort, I will double it." Too often pastors are so busy with managing ministries, participating in meetings, and maintaining the facilities that they are unable to spend quality time throughout the week preparing food (the sermon) as nourishment for people on Sunday.

Without the influence of the Holy Spirit, a sermon is simply an inspirational message. On the other hand, under the influence of the Holy Spirit, a sermon is a power-packed transformational instrument that feeds Jesus's sheep exactly what they need. A preacher's true anointing can only come from God. It is only under the power of God through the Holy Spirit that a preacher is able to reveal, in a relevant way, God's plan for humanity. That's why the sermon preparation time is not just a time to study but also a time to spend with God, listening, discerning, and receiving. James Forbes (pastor emeritus of Riverside Church in New York) contends, "Only by the anointing of the Spirit does the vision of God's kingdom become so etched in the mind and heart that action must flow from it. Only through anointed preachers will death and its structure of oppression be exposed for what they really are."[5] Just as there cannot be powerful preaching without the Holy Spirit, there cannot be accurate receiving of the message without the influence of the Spirit. It has been said many times before and in a number of different ways: preaching is the responsibility of the preacher and the hearers. The pastor preaches and the people pray. It goes hand in hand.

Furthermore, I think people come to the preaching moment on Sunday hungry. They are looking for something that will address their concerns, fears, and hopes. The hunger that people feel might be the result of any number of things, including a busy workweek, the pressure of paying bills, familial challenges, or personal temptations. All of those things can weigh on a person, or, in other words, drain the life out of them. That leads to a feeling of being depleted, and the only way to get out of this rut is to have something fill them back up. They are looking for something that will reenergize them to go back out and face the world again, one more week. So they go to the church house on Sunday morning expecting a word from God, through the pastor, that will satisfy the longing inside them.

The anointing power of the Spirit gives the power and blessing to do what God has called one to do. More than anything, that anointing means believing that because God has called one to preach God has equipped one to do so. When a pastor believes God has equipped him or her, preaching becomes a bold declaration during which the Spirit endows the preacher with confidence to proclaim the good news of Jesus Christ. Jesus promised his apostles that the same power they saw in him would be available to them through the Holy Spirit. That's why Peter, on the Day of Pentecost, was able to declare with certainty the saving power of Jesus the Christ. So much so that three thousand souls ate (bread of heaven) so well that they gave themselves to the Lord on that day (Acts 2). As pastors, we are also able to use that power from the Holy Spirit to proclaim throughout the world that Jesus is Lord with the same energy and passion that Peter possessed on the Day of Pentecost. Peter gave them the word and they were satisfied.

Let me explain what I mean when I say the word, because it is the word of God that holds the preaching together. Without being too abstract, the word is what God spoke when all things were created, and the word is what holds all of creation in order. Not only that, but the word was the means by which all things came into existence. The Word is the truth and power of God, which entered human history in the person of Jesus of Nazareth.

Throughout the centuries God has spoken to humanity. The word of God has always been with humankind, directing us in the right path. It is how God moves God's people from one place to the next. God's word came to Abram, instructing him to leave his homeland to go to a new place. Through God's word Moses was instructed to tell Pharaoh and convince the Israelites that it was time to leave Egypt for a new place that God had for them. In the same manner, it is through the word of God given to the pastor that congregations discover what the next phase of ministry and worship is for that particular community of faith. Churches come to know how to live and where it is God is leading them through God's word spoken to and through individuals, especially the shepherd of the church.

Perhaps today more than ever, as pastors it is our calling to proclaim God's word. That's what the world needs to hear and it is exactly what God calls pastors to do. It is how pastors feed God's sheep on a consistent basis. God uses the pastor as an instrument to declare the truth, which is Jesus, in order to bring about conversion and transformation in the lives of the hearers. Pastors of the gospel participate in the reshaping, redemptive, and life-giving action of the word by sharing the word as it is revealed through the power of the Holy Spirit. Therefore, just like a marriage, preaching should "not be entered into unadvisedly, but reverently, discreetly, and in the fear of God."[6]

Pastors of the gospel participate in the reshaping, redemptive, and life-giving action of the word by sharing the word as it is revealed through the power of the Holy Spirit.

People cannot do unless they first know. They cannot know unless someone shares knowledge with them. The preaching ministry of the pastor is the most powerful and effective way to feed a large number of sheep at once. Without this mass feeding process called preaching, how will the sheep know what they have been charged to do? The Apostle Paul put it this way: "How can they call on someone they don't have faith in? And how can they have faith in someone they haven't heard of? And how can they hear without a preacher?" (Romans 10:14)

Now that we have established that preaching is the primary way in which pastors feed the flock, let me try to summarize how the feeding should be done. Pastors are to proclaim God's truth and teach how it is to be lived out. In the twenty-first century the gospel message has to be offered in a way that people will readily receive it. The food presented to Jesus's sheep in a sermon must be grace filled, easily understood, life enhancing, and saturated with hope.

Early on in my ministry, Gene Lowry (emeritus preaching professor at Saint Paul School of Theology) told me the same thing he used to share with my father: make sure the sermon points to God's grace. After all, the foundation of our faith rests upon God's free gift of love found in Christ Jesus. That's why it is essential that the recipients of the sermon understand that redemption, forgiveness, and wholeness are possible only because of the unmerited gift of God's love. I know we want sermons to have catchy titles and be filled with memorable sound bites, but without grace the message fails to be a sermon. It is merely a motivational speech with religious overtones. We are saved by grace, and that's exactly what people need to hear week after week, either implicitly or explicitly. People should leave the worship experience knowing and believing that God loves them unconditionally.

We are saved by grace, and that's exactly what people need to hear

86

week after week, either implicitly or explicitly.

While highlighting God's undeserved love is the most important aspect of the sermon, it is all for nothing if people don't understand it. Perhaps at one time in American history people were more biblically literate and had a greater comprehension of Christian concepts and terminology. Unfortunately, today that is not the case. We live in a society where people did not grow up in a church, and even those who did don't seem to be very biblically knowledgeable. Therefore, pastors have to remember that feeding sheep may require more explanations of biblical stories and Christian concepts. We cannot assume that when we use a word such as *justification* people will know what it means. We can't make reference to the Twenty-Third Psalm and the Lord's Prayer and assume that everyone in the congregation knows what we are talking about. No matter how much a pastor prays and studies, if the gospel message isn't presented in a manner that is easily understood, the pastor has missed the mark. Sheep, especially those new in the faith, typically won't eat if they don't know what they are eating. Stated another way, how can people receive food of the gospel if it is too complicated to understand?

If the gospel message isn't presented in a manner that is easily understood, the pastor has missed the mark.

The message also has to be life enhancing. In other words, the sermon should provide practical ways in which someone's life can become better while in relationship with Jesus. Provide applicable answers that help people grow deeper in their faith. The gospel is more than simply providing information and giving nice illustrations. People truly want to know what those biblical stories have to do with their lives today. What good is a sermon if it does not offer listeners anything they can actually apply when they leave the church house on Sunday? The sermon should offer something that helps to enhance the lives of those who receive the bread from heaven.

The gospel message should be not only grace filled, easily understood, and life enhancing, but also saturated with hope. So many people in our world are hurting from the stress and strain of living on this side of the grave. Many people are out of work, in debt, or struggling in their marriages, and they are looking for something to hold on to. Something that helps them face tomorrow with the confidence that things can and will get better. People need and want to know that their current predicaments, whatever they might be, are not permanent. Jesus preached about something better that was at hand and would later be fully realized in the kingdom of God. So it makes sense that pastors today would do the same. Preach as though someone's livelihood depends on it.

I cannot stress enough how important preaching is for the healing, wholeness, and vitality of a faith community. Preaching is not the only time in which people's souls can be fed. There should be other growing opportunities like Bible studies, small groups, church school, and so on.

However, for many people, preaching is their only faith-development opportunity all week. No matter how well attended our other church activities are it is in worship where we have our largest gathering of people each week.

Questions for Reflection

1. How seriously is preaching taken in your church?

2. How can a congregation help with the sermon preparation and the preaching moment each week?

3. How much time should a pastor spend preparing a sermon?

4. Does your church have any other time during the week (outside of Sunday) to discuss and review the sermon?

5. What are the elements of a good sermon?

6. Are most of your sermons grace filled, easily understood, life enhancing and saturated with hope?

Chapter 7

The Work of the People

You yourselves are being built like living stones into a spiritual temple. You are being made into a holy priesthood to offer up spiritual sacrifices that are acceptable to God through Jesus Christ.

—1 Peter 2:5

The purpose of the church of Jesus Christ is to continue the work of Jesus in transforming the world by making disciples. The responsibility of the body of Christ is to make disciples for Jesus Christ to the glory of God the Father. That's where the leadership, vision, and teaching of the pastor come into play. All believers must understand the purpose of their gifts of the Spirit and how they work together for the good of God's church. It is through our God-given gifts that we are enabled to accomplish the purpose of the church.

In a world where pain, suffering, and natural disaster are normal parts of life, there is always a need for comfort and hope. When oppression and discrimination rear their ugly heads in the forms of racism, classism, and sexism on a daily basis, there is a need for justice. In a society that gives the impression of being on the side of the rich and stepping over the poor, there is a need for compassion. Lifeforms cannot run from the inevitable clutches of death and the grief caused by it; there is a need for hope! It is in this context that the church must fulfill its calling and purpose.

There are, without question, a plethora of areas in which the church is needed to provide the hope and security that many souls are searching for. Ministry, I believe, must be at the forefront of the local church's life. People who are hungry, who are literally suffering from daily hunger pangs, care more about having their needs met than they do about hearing of a loving God. If the local church is going to be a vital institution in our communities across this nation and the world, it must carry out the business of service. That begins with God-given guidance and direction from the one placed over the congregation, the pastor. If the church is to be of any assistance to the lost, the left out, the seekers, and even the morally bankrupt, then it must first gain a proper understanding of what ministry is, and who is responsible for carrying it out. This is the reason it is important not just to understand the role of the pastor but to explore the calling, purpose, and meaning of ministry for and by the people.

> # It is important not just to understand the role of the pastor but to explore the calling, purpose, and meaning of ministry for and by the people.

Whose Job Is It, Anyway?

As I shared earlier, lay members in congregations I have served have expressed both directly and indirectly that if a church is going to have any type of ministries, they must and should be formed and performed by the pastor. When I have explained that the pastor's role is to give vision and to equip others to help reach that vision and that ministry is to be done by parishioners, I have received strange looks, as if I were speaking a foreign language. It appears to me that either we clergy are not emphasizing in our teachings that service to the world is the calling of every member of the body of Christ or the laity have not accepted this teaching. Perhaps it is a combination of both. Pastors don't drive the point home out of fear of shaking things up, and laity don't accept it because it doesn't fit their cultural and historical understanding of the role of the pastor. Whatever the reason for this confusion, the entire church must realize that we have been mandated by God to share the good news of Jesus Christ through word and deed. "All members are called to offer their being as a living sacrifice to intercede for Church and for the world."[1] Because the Holy Spirit has endowed all believers with gifts, we all have a responsibility to use our gifts in service to the world.[2] With all the problems facing our world, it makes little sense to place the responsibility of addressing these concerns on one person per community of faith. Each member of the church must step up to the plate and use what God has given him or her in order to advance the kingdom of God on earth. God does not give believers gifts for the sake of giving gifts. Each member of the church must be taught— and it should become a part of each congregation's culture—that no one person makes up a church. Instead, the church is made up of individuals, and they must go and serve the world both individually and collectively.

Each member of the church must
be taught—and it should become
a part of each congregation's
culture—that no one person
makes up a church. Instead, the
church is made up of individuals,

93

and they must go and serve the world both individually and collectively.

The purpose of church ministry, simply put, is to continue the work Jesus began. Jesus ushered in an era of compassion, justice, and love. What makes Jesus's ministry so amazing is that he addressed the social, physical, emotional, and spiritual needs of people. We are, as the body of Christ, the representatives of Jesus in the world today. When Jesus ascended into heaven, he passed the torch of kingdom building on to his disciples, and they passed the torch on to future generations. The astonishing thing is that Jesus did not develop a backup plan for bringing humanity back to God. Jesus trusts and believes that his followers will live up to their mandate and accomplish what he started. We, the church, have been given the responsibility of preaching the gospel to the poor, healing the brokenhearted, offering ease and comfort to those struggling with emotional issues, and providing understanding to the confused. Above and beyond anything else, the church is called to be in service to the world.

In order to carry out this calling, the church and local congregations must be directed onto the right path. Congregations require a conductor to be in charge—to keep them on track. As part of the body of Christ, the conductors/pastors are called to provide leadership and guidance in our churches. Every generation is able to continue and expand the ministry of the church because of the authority and tradition passed down for the purpose of providing a standard that the church should follow. The World Council of Churches' commission on faith and order believes, "The Spirit keeps the Church in the apostolic tradition until the fulfillment of history in the Kingdom of God."[3] All believers are called to serve. However, there are those who are called to be set apart to lead, teach, instruct, and direct the church—keeping the church on track. Pastors in every congregation are set apart to "assemble and guide the dispersed people of God, in anticipation of the coming Kingdom."[4]

Pastors have an important responsibility and awesome task in directing the affairs of the church (1 Timothy 5:17). Although pastors and laity alike have a role in the church, those roles are different. I want to be clear that the difference in roles does not mean pastors are better than laity; however, it might imply that pastors must not enter into their calling lightly but prayerfully and in the fear of God. Both roles in our churches are important. Spiritual gifts are given to laity for the sake of advancing the mission of the church. But the office of pastor is a gift that God has given to the church. Pastors are the gift to every congregation sent to encourage people to follow in the footsteps of Jesus by promoting, justice, peace, and service to the world.

The pastor has the role of overseeing and working in not just one area of ministry but all areas, taking a bird's-eye view of ministry rather than an on-the-ground view.

The pastor has the role of overseeing and working in not just one area of ministry but all areas, taking a bird's-eye view of ministry rather than an on-the-ground view. I have discovered that everyone believes the area of ministry they are working in deserves a great deal of attention from the pastor. While individuals understand the importance of other ministry areas, their focus is on what *they* are doing. Thus, that particular ministry becomes the most important thing in the church to them. The pastor cannot take this position.

He or she must understand that all areas of ministry are important and show appreciation for the value of all the ministries. Part of the pastor's role in casting the vision and equipping the saints is to help each member of the body of Christ not only understand his or her own gifts, but to understand the purpose of all spiritual gifts in and of themselves. Pastors must teach the congregants about the church's other ministries and how the gifts and ministries of others in the church are important and useful, too. Further, we must teach our congregations correctly about the role of pastor. We must begin to correct the widespread misunderstanding in churches of this role, and guide our parishioners to understand God's intention for the ordained leaders of the church.

Unleashing the Gifts of the Spirit in Our Congregations

The purpose of gifts of the Spirit is to glorify the body of Christ. This is done in three ways: (1) unifying the body, (2) enabling the believers for ministry, and (3) perfecting the saints.[5]

Gifts of Unity

In the twelfth chapter of his Letter to the Romans, Paul expresses the need for believers to seek unity with one another, and he explains that God's gifts of grace are key components in facilitating that unity. A body's parts must be of one accord if the body is to achieve its goals and objectives. New Testament scholar N.T. Wright puts it this way: "In particular, in the Messiah Christians are to strive for unity, which will come through the humility in which each thinks soberly about his or her own gifts rather than placing too high value on them."[6] Each believer receives his or her gifts from the same source, the Holy Spirit, and that source unifies us. These gifts are not trophies to show off, which consequently brings division. Our spiritual gifts are for the general excellence of the entire community of faith.[7] Gifts, though different, are all connected to one another in that they come from the same source and serve the same ultimate purpose. That's why the effective practice of a gift is directly linked to the effective practice of other gifts and the believers that posses them. As the shepherd of a congregation, a pastor must preach and teach the unity of believers as it relates to our gifts.

Gifts of Empowerment

Spiritual gifts also glorify the body of Christ by empowering and equipping believers to carry out the ministry of the church. I talked about this in a previous chapter, but I want to reiterate how important it is for the church to understand this. In order for the pastor to live out his calling, members need to understand their function. The effectiveness of a church is directly linked to the pastor's understanding of his or her role as well as each member of the community knowing their responsibilities. That's why gifts of the Spirit are so important when it comes to the life of a congregation. One could even say that gifts of the Spirit give us an idea as to what our ministerial tasks should be. How that is carried out depends on the context of the community and the personality of each particular believer. Our gifts do often lead us toward the kind of service God is calling us to, and thus one's spiritual gifts are vital in determining what God's calling is on one's life. If God gives us each a function, God also equips us with what we need to accomplish it. When we live in accordance with our God-given gifts, our service becomes more efficient and effective, bringing glory to the body of Christ.

Gifts of Growth

The third way in which gifts build up the body of Christ is by helping us grow in the love and knowledge of Jesus Christ. This means walking and talking in the same compassion, sincerity, and truth as Jesus. Because Jesus is the standard by which we measure our faith, becoming like him should be our ultimate goal. I believe it is necessary to look at this third point in two ways: individual faith development and communal maturity.

Growth as Individuals

As individual stewards of God's gifts, we must understand and accept that God's intent is that we not remain the same but rather allow our gifts to help us grow in the love of Jesus. The Holy Spirit's gifts practiced in the believer produce Christlike behavior and results: "The primary work of the Holy Spirit is to make us like Jesus. He gives spiritual gifts *to* us so that we can do the work of Christ, and produces spiritual fruit *in* us so that we can look and act like Christ. Because He is the Spirit of Christ, He reproduces the life of Christ in us."[8] This is to say that gifts are not only for doing but also for becoming. That's why many make the connection between spiritual gifts and the fruit of the Spirit.

But the fruit of the Spirit is love, joy, peace, patience, kindness, goodness, faithfulness, gentleness, and self-control. There is no law against things like this. (Galatians 5:22-23)

Charles Hummel makes the argument, and rightfully so, that the fruit of the Spirit and the gifts of the Spirit are different. The fruit is meant for every believer, while gifts vary from believer to believer. Fruit is about being, while gifts are more about doing.[9] A gift is an attribute, and the fruit deals more with a person's character. While the two are different, I agree with Carlyle Stewart that our gifts are used by the Spirit to produce fruit of the Spirit within us.[10] Hummel does note that there is a connection between the two found in 1 Corinthians 13, Paul's classic writing on love.[11] The love of God empowers us to apply our gifts that produce spiritual fruit. In other words, having the Holy Spirit operate in us through gifts brings about transformation to the believer. The gifts of the Spirit enhance and preserve Christian character.[12] The same Spirit that empowers us to do ministry also produces the fruit within us. The fruit of the Spirit are perhaps greater evidence of the Holy Spirit's presence than spiritual gifts.[13] While it is true that the Holy Spirit is constantly producing fruit in the lives of believers, the Spirit also uses our gifts to fertilize and enhance that fruit.

98

Growth as a Community

The second way gifts of the Spirit perfect the saints is by nurturing the body of Christ as a whole toward Christian maturity. The entire community of faith is called to operate together in the same power and knowledge of Christ. Individual growth plays a role in the growth of the body; however, the body is not complete in one individual's growth alone.[14] No one individual can act as the eyes, hands, and mouth of Jesus; it is only the collective body of saints that represents Christ's presence in the world today. Thomas Neufeld says, "Whereas the church is 'already' the *fullness* of Christ ([Ephesians] 1:23), its ministry is geared to having it arrive at a *fullness* that is 'not yet' perfect."[15] The sense here is that while believers make up the body of Christ, we have not yet become in full what we've been called to be. This is why the role of the pastor is so important for the health, vitality, and future of the church.

> # No one individual can act as the eyes, hands, and mouth of Jesus; it is only the collective body of saints that represents Christ's presence in the world today.

One's personal gifts cannot be used to their full potential without cooperation with the rest of the body. For instance, an individual playing a team sport cannot use his or her abilities to their fullest without the assistance of the rest of the team. The saying "There is no *I* in team" is worthy of full acceptance. While Christian maturity is the goal of every believer, it cannot be attained without living in and sharing with the entire body.[16] It is through our gifts that we can become more like Christ together. We are able to carry out our

Christian mandates and loyally serve as Christ's representatives in the world when we use our gifts jointly within a faith community. The cooperative application of gifts fosters growth for the entire community. Neufeld goes on to say, "The *saints* must be conscious of the fact that they must draw on the *gifts* of Christ to live up to their identity as Christ's body, and to grow more fully into that identity."[17] The body lives into its identity only when the pastor lives into his or her identity.

Reclaiming Our Identity: Pastors *and* Congregations

Why does all this matter? Why is it so important that the church understand spiritual gifts in order to understand the true role of a pastor? The reason is because pastors cannot reclaim their identity unless all the people of God reclaim their roles and responsibilities as equipped members of the body of Christ. If the church is going to be effective in fulfilling its purpose of making disciples for Jesus Christ, ministry cannot be viewed as something the pastor does alone. God has established roles for laity and clergy alike, and when people operate in their roles, we are able to accomplish exactly what God has called us to do and be.

> God has established roles for laity and clergy alike, and when people operate in their roles, we are able to accomplish exactly what God has called us to do and be.

As the body of Christ our purpose is to grow into the fullness of Christ's power, knowledge, and love through the gifts of the Spirit.

The body of Christ is glorified through the ministries of the church, unity among believers, and the corporate and individual maturity in Jesus by way of God's gifts of grace. The only way that comes to fruition is if the pastor understands his or her identity. The pastor must step out of the misconceptions of the office and step into the true identity of "ministry enabler" by way of preaching, teaching, training, and pointing the train in the right direction for the future.

> # An essential function of the pastor is to equip the people so that they can operate in accordance with their God-given gifts.

The pastor builds the body of Christ by helping its members understand who they are in that body and by helping them grow in the love and knowledge of Christ. An essential function of the pastor is to equip the people so that they can operate in accordance with their God-given gifts. The church of Jesus Christ cannot accomplish its purpose unless the gift to each church, the pastor, is living in his or her purpose, equipping the saints. The ministry of those saints will accomplish God's purpose for the earth.

Reclaiming Our Authority: The Pastor as Priest and Elder

Modern Christians may be shocked to know that in the early days of the church, pastors were viewed with a great deal of respect as the authority in local congregations. It seems that the word *authority* has a negative connotation in the minds of some people today, at least in North America. They hear the word and they associate it with a boss, dictator, or some kind of ruler. It is especially hard for those of us living in a democratic society. We believe that a nation operates best when it puts things to a vote and the majority wins. Whatever the majority decides is what we ought to do. Well, in government the majority may decide, but the majority is not always right. I'm not suggesting that the United States ought to do away with democracy. I believe it is the best form of government in the world. However, I'm not sure God intended the church to be a democracy. On the other hand, I don't believe God intended congregations to be run by a dictator. I do believe that God desires for the church to be Christ centered and Christ driven. But what does that mean for a congregation today? Should a congregation be run like a democracy or is there a different and better model?

I've often wondered if Jesus intended for the church to be a democracy. The Catholic church for centuries has said no, while in mainline Protestant congregations democracy is a part of the structure. But what is the biblical model of organizational control and pastoral authority? We do see in the Old and New Testaments that God established the leadership and God's vision through leaders. These leaders served as representatives or the mouthpiece of God. The prophets and high priests were viewed as the authoritative figures anointed and appointed by God. So when a prophet or a priest spoke, the people believed that he was speaking on behalf of God. Since the high priest was considered a God-sanctioned authority, the people listened and followed. The high priest did not have to run anything past a board or any other person. If, by way of the Urim and Thummim, some word came from the Lord, the people trusted it, believed it, and followed it.

While the people accepted the authority of the priest, it was not as though others who belonged to the people of God were not given any say. There were the elders, who were respected and looked to for guidance and wisdom. However, when it came to carrying out the rules as given by God, that was the high priest's responsibility. There is a place for others besides the pastors to serve and participate in leadership in the church, but the pastor does have God-given authority.

102

In the New Testament I think we have even more of an example of authority and church polity. The elders (which in many traditions are the same as pastors) are called to oversee the dealings of the local congregation. I take that to mean the elders/pastors are to give the vision for the congregation and lead them into that vision. It does not suggest that the elders/pastors must get approval or even a vote from the leaders of the congregation. As I stated in a previous chapter, I truly believe it would stifle the leadership of the pastor if he or she had to get approval when it came to casting a vision for the church.

While the vision must be accepted and embraced by the congregation, it is my belief that God gives the vision to the pastor to share with the rest of the community of faith. First, vision should come from the pastor and not a committee, because this fits with the biblical model of God giving the vision to the man or woman of God. Second, to a point I made earlier, settling on a vision would be a very long process, and people would have to concede some of their ideas to satisfy the group. I would contend that a vision put together by a committee would be convoluted, incoherent, and confused. The vision would have several threads from several people, making it more of a multivision than a single vision. Third, if a pastor is preaching and teaching a vision that he "received" from a committee, he is preaching on something that may or may not have come from God. This reduces the authority of the pastor and, perhaps, the congregation's view of the authority of God.

This does not mean that people other than the pastor don't have influence or input in the life of a congregation. Nothing could be further from the truth. When the pastor, by way of the authority of the office, sets the vision, she or he then gives ministry leaders and the governing board an opportunity to be creative and come up with innovative ideas to carry out the vision. Again, some pastors may guide congregational leaders in the visioning process. This is perfectly fine, in my view, as long as it is the pastor who is leading the process. When the leaders of the congregation accept the pastor's God-given authority, true leadership and ministry can take place.

I think it is difficult for people in many congregations today to receive the word *authority*. As mentioned earlier, North American churchgoers may not be willing to accept the authority of the pastor because we are so accustomed to a democratic process. But the authority of the pastor is rooted in the biblical tradition, which should trump North American culture and tradition. God's people have always had leaders who direct, protect, and nurture the community of faith. We see that authority played out through elders in the Old Testament, the priests, kings, and later the apostles. The authority of the pastor is much deeper than a congregation's understanding, denominational expectations, and cultural norms. It is given and secured by the ultimate authority, God. I believe it is important for pastors and congregations to accept that. If parishioners cannot accept the authority of the pastor's role, they will be less likely to accept the pastor's teaching and preaching on the vision of the church. Likewise, if the pastor does not claim his or her own authority, he or she may lack the confidence required to cast that vision in the first place. However, when the leadership of the church and the entire congregation understands and accepts the pastor's God-given authority to lead the congregation, the entire church will move more smoothly toward fulfilling its purpose. The train will stay on track with forward momentum. The congregants know where to look and who to talk to about where it is they are going and what it is they are trying to accomplish as a community of faith. The pastor's power and influence is not based on education or personality. It is based on the truth that God has endowed the office of pastor with authority. The ministry of a church is effective when the members of the body understand, accept, and embrace this fact.

To pastors I would ask, "How can you proclaim the truth unless you believe you have the authority to do so?" To laity I would ask, "Why would you listen to what the pastor teaches if you don't believe he or she has the authority to teach it?" Walter E. Wiest and Elwyn A. Smith say it like this in their book *Ethics in Ministry*: "The authority of the clergy is not its own; it is Christ's and is conveyed by the gospel entrusted to the church."[18] The effectiveness of the pastor's teaching, preaching, visioning, and leading rests upon his or her willingness to claim this God-given authority. When I was ordained an elder in The United Methodist Church in 2003, Bishop Ann Sherer (now Sherer-Simpson) told me and the other ordinands to "take thou authority." The authority ordained by God, made evident in Jesus, continued through the apostles by way of the Holy Spirit, entrusted to the church, and passed down to each generation. I want to remind all pastors and inform laity that the pastor has been commissioned by God with the authority to feed God's sheep and lead them into greener pastures.

Questions for Reflection

1. How does your church understand and treat spiritual gifts?

2. What does it mean that the office of pastor is God's gift to the church?

3. How can your church implement a program for spiritual gifts?

4. Why is it important for the pastor to equip church members for ministry?

5. What are some opportunities your church has available for the pastor to equip and empower members for ministry?

Chapter 8

Essential: Discern
God's Will

If you can hear, listen to what the Spirit is saying to the churches.
—*Revelation 3:6*

The Care and Feeding of a Pastor's Soul

Someone once said, "If you see a Buddhist monk, you see a holy man. If you see a pastor, you see a manager." A holy disposition only comes from spending quality time with the Holy One. In order to effectively feed God's sheep, the pastor must first feed himself or herself. It is critical that pastors spend time alone with the Lord feasting on God's truth in order to adequately feed the congregation. How can you feed another when you are hungry yourself? Even pastors hunger for answers, guidance, purpose, and meaning in life. We hunger for wisdom, knowledge, and understanding just like everyone else. The problem is that unless we satisfy the hunger that all humans experience by spending time with God in prayer and meditating on scripture, it is nearly impossible to feed those we have been charged to care for.

This point is made every time we fly on an airplane. Before we take off, the flight attendant makes a speech to this effect: "In the case of a loss of cabin pressure, oxygen masks will fall from the ceiling. Place the

107

oxygen mask over your mouth and nose and breathe normally. If you are flying with small children or with others who may need assistance, please place the oxygen mask on yourself first before assisting others." Airlines know that if you can't breathe and you are trying to help someone else, all you will end up doing is hurting yourself and the one you are trying to assist. It's not selfish to put the mask on first; rather, it is prudent and has the potential to save multiple lives.

Likewise, it is not selfish for pastors to take care of themselves and spend quality time alone with God. Rather, it is generous and practical to set aside time to feed your soul with prayer, fasting, searching scriptures, and silence before God. How else do we expect to hear from God as to what direction we should aim the train, what we should proclaim to the people, and where we should lead them?

We pastors must first take care of our own souls or we will find ourselves drained and spiritually depleted, becoming ever more desperate to find nourishment when we should be focused on nourishing others. Imagine going to a soup kitchen to feed the hungry, but you have not eaten. You are hungry, and soon you find that you are easily distracted from your work. It is not unreasonable to assume that you would start craving the very food you are supposed to give others. You might even start nibbling on the food and feeding yourself while ignoring those in line.

We pastors must first take care of our own souls or we will find ourselves drained and spiritually depleted, becoming ever more desperate to find nourishment when we should be focused on nourishing others.

It is for this reason that the majority of the pastor's week should be spent in prayer and study so that he or she can be fed and then feed others. Jesus was a perfect example of this. He would often get away from his followers to spend quality time alone with his Father. Once his soul had been cultivated, Jesus would then go and share with others what he had received from the Father. He even began his earthly ministry by feasting on the words from his Father as he spent alone time out in the desert. After his alone time feeding his soul, Jesus would go back to his assignment of empowering and equipping his disciples to transform the world. So too should pastors spend alone time nourishing our souls so we can feed others.

Quality time alone with the Lord is not only for pastors; it is also critical for church board members, staff, ministry leaders, and the entire congregation. The pastor will never be able to devote time to study and prayer if the congregants do not understand and embrace that practice—for the pastor and for themselves. The pastor's time will quickly fill up with meetings, counseling, visitations, and so on if the church leaders don't understand the role and importance of the pastor seeking alone time with God. The laity will not support—and may even come to resent—the pastor's prioritization of study and prayer. We not only must teach this prioritization for our lay leaders, we must model it.

The pastor will never be able to devote time to study and prayer if the congregants do not understand and embrace that practice—for the pastor and for themselves.

Through focused prayer and time with God, the pastor's sermon preparation becomes more than an academic exercise; it becomes a spiritual experience. Zan Holmes once commented that when the message touches him during his sermon preparation, he knows it will touch others. Imagine that—being filled while preparing for a sermon. Many pastors dread preparing a sermon. They like preaching, but preparing is another story. However, the preparation time will take on an entirely new meaning if viewed as an opportunity to grow closer to God and deeper in our commitment. When study and prayer go together, God's will is then made manifest through the teaching and preaching preparation. Many pastors already do spend significant time in focused study and prayer as part of their sermon preparation each week, but perhaps this serves as a reminder for other pastors who have become complacent or weary or otherwise off track.

The preparation time will take on an entirely new meaning if viewed as an opportunity to grow closer to God and deeper in our commitment.

The Power of Being Alone

Pastors must intentionally step away from meetings, agendas, distractions, and people to simply listen to God. We see people time and again in the Bible who are away from everyone and everything else when receiving a word from the Lord so they can share it with others. Remember that it was when Moses was tending his father-in-law's sheep that he heard from God. Moses was alone, no people, no cell phones, no MP3 player, and no distractions at all when God gave him instructions to share with the enslaved Hebrews. That would then become a part of Moses's regular practice, to get away from everyone and spend time with the Lord. It was up on the mountaintop, away from the Hebrew camp, the grumblings of the people, and even his family that God gave Moses the Ten Commandments. Moses was alone with God on Mount Sinai so that he could properly instruct and lead the people.

We can see the importance of quality time alone with God in the story of Samuel. Samuel was alone in the house of the Lord when he heard the voice of God in the middle of the night. It was that alone time that gave him clarity, courage, and conviction to lead God's people from a system of judges to a system of kings. Samuel had quality time with the Lord, and thus God's people could see God's power and presence in him just as with Moses.

We see in Isaiah chapter 6 that the prophet Isaiah's calling into the ministry of the Lord occurred in similar fashion. Isaiah was all alone in the temple when he received not only his calling but also his instructions for ministry. Isaiah did some talking in that alone time with the Lord, but he also listened so that he could properly and effectively communicate to the people he was called to lead. The quiet time with God fed Isaiah's soul so that in turn he could go out and feed others. God still speaks to us today and God definitely speaks to, instructs, and feeds pastors so that they can effectively lead God's people. We just have to make sure we intentionally set aside time to talk to and listen to the Lord.

If we pastors are going to get back on track, we must begin with scheduling a significant amount of time during the workweek to hear from God. That quality time should not simply be the pastor praying and asking God for directions but rather listening and discerning what God is actually saying. Notice in 1 Samuel 3 when the priest Eli informed Samuel that it was God speaking to him, Eli told the young boy to allow God to do all the talking. Too often, even as pastors, we thank God, ask God, and praise God in our prayers, but we forget to listen to God.

Hearing from God

One question that often comes up whenever there is talk about listening to God is: How does God talk to us? There are a number of different ways in which we can hear God speaking. Sometimes it is something deep within us that goes beyond a feeling or anxiousness. I've heard people refer to it as "something in my spirit." When this comes over a person, they often believe it is God speaking to them. I know others who receive their instructions from God by journaling. They keep a daily record of what happens in their lives and how, where, and when God shows up. They review that daily record to see how God is speaking to them.

There are many different ways we hear from God. I'm not sure one way is better than another. What is most important is that pastors daily seek to hear from God regarding their personal lives and where God is calling them to move their congregations. At one point in my ministry I struggled with discerning God's will for the congregation I was serving. Because I wasn't always clear on what God was saying to me, I led based on my own assumptions and thoughts or on what I had read. In my early days of ministry I had not really developed a way to truly hear from God. I knew to pray, which I did often; I just did not know how to listen. Through the course of time and the necessity to lead God's people more effectively, I found a method of hearing from God that suited my style of praying. It was something that was right in front of me the entire time.

I adapted the *lectio divina* form of praying as a means to hear God clearly speak to me in my personal life as well as in the life of the congregation. This is an ancient form of prayer and meditation whereby you seek to hear from God regarding your personal life through scripture. When I am trying to discern where God wants me to lead the congregation or even my personal life, I meditate on scripture. I pray and ask God for clarity on a ministry, a teaching series, worship, or the overall direction of the church. My prayer is centered around hearing from God on that particular church-related issue. I then open the Bible and read whatever page I have randomly opened it to. I believe and trust that God is in the midst of the process and has directed me to the exact page and has led my eyes to the specific passage through which God will speak to me. I do this not looking for a sermon idea or Bible study but trying to hear God's voice. I meditate on that particular scripture believing that God will reveal to me what I need to know in order to equip and lead the congregation as the senior pastor. Of course, just like any spiritual discipline, it takes some time and practice to truly identify how and what God is saying to you through scripture as it relates to ministry and leadership. That's how I hear God, but other pastors may hear from God in entirely different manners. The method that we use to receive instructions from God for our ministries is not particularly important. What matters most is that pastors discover a way in which they can clearly hear God speaking to them. When that's accomplished, pastors have to make sure they take the time on a regular basis to listen to the voice of God.

The method that we use to receive instructions from God for our ministries is not particularly important. What matters most is that pastors discover a way in which they can clearly hear God speaking to them.

Sharing What You Hear

Once I am certain that I have heard from God, I then begin putting the plan in place. I first share the vision with the staff so that they understand where God is leading us. Once the staff is on board, we share it with the appropriate ministry leaders. When the leaders are in unison and understand the vision that God has given me, we can truly implement the plan. The process all begins with hearing from God. Furthermore, I think it is important for pastors to let church leaders and the congregation as a whole know that what they are doing is not an opinion and not necessarily what the pastor wants to do. What they are doing is what the pastor believes God wants them to do.

Questions for Reflection

1. How important is alone time with the Lord in your faith journey?

2. How often do we as pastors teach and preach on self-care?

3. What are some ways in which you can clearly hear God speaking to you?

4. What other biblical examples can you think of when someone was alone and they heard God speak?

5. Is your prayer time spent mostly talking or listening? How do you listen to God in your prayer time?

Chapter 9

Making Change: Pastoral Examples (Time on the Mountain)

The LORD said to Moses, "Come up to me on the mountain and wait there. I'll give you the stone tablets with the instructions and the commandments that I've written in order to teach them."
—Exodus 24:12

While I do believe pastoral ministry has gotten off track to a certain degree, there are many women and men staying true to the biblical job description of pastor. We have examined five essential functions of the pastor—casting the vision, leading the people, developing staff and lay leaders around the vision, teaching and preaching, and discerning God's will. The final function is most critical, and none of the other functions can happen without it. It is, however, probably the function with which many of us struggle the most. Thus, I thought it was important to end this book by giving some examples of pastors who are able to get away from the church building, not necessarily out of town, simply to find a quiet place to be with God. These pastors are able to spend quality time with the Lord in order to discern where it is God is leading their particular congregation. I wanted to share modern ministry models in which pastors plan out where a congregation is going when it comes to sermons, ministries, themes for various events, and the overall direction. This is what I call mountaintop time. When Moses went up to Mount Sinai it was just he and the Lord. When Moses came down he presented the people with a vision and plan called the Ten Commandments.

Because I know so many pastors across denominational lines, I initially thought about sending out a message asking pastors to share their stories. Over and over again pastors have told me they want to do that sort of planning, to intentionally reorder their time, to reclaim their true roles as pastors. Many of us seem to plan on doing it someday, but we find it is easier said than done. Several pastors told me that though they had heard about other pastors who were beginning to operate differently by focusing on the essential functions of the pastor, they were unable to find the time or capacity to begin making those changes themselves. They expressed how time alone with God, especially, would make their ministries more purposeful and clear. Yet it was not a very common thing, I discovered, for pastors to isolate themselves from everything and everyone but God in order to discern what was next. Life as a pastor focused on these essentials seems to exist in a mythical place that pastors have read about in fairy tales and heard seminary professors talk about rather than in "real life."

For years I was among the pastors who dreamed of spending a few days, a week perhaps, planning out what was next for the congregation I serve. It finally happened when my executive assistant, Tracy Milsap, blocked out two weeks on my calendar. She did not schedule any appointments, meetings, or other obligations so that I could get out of the church building and spend quality time with the Lord. Those two weeks were spent at the Saint Paul School of Theology library in a quiet study carrel, where I heard from God. This is now a practice that I do two to three times a year. I was able to discern what the theme would be for the year and put together sermon titles with scripture and a basic outline for an entire quarter.

118

God also showed me during that time events, teaching series, and new initiatives for the next four to six months. When I got back to my study after two weeks away, I was able to share with the staff where God was leading St. James.

We had a theme to base our special celebrations around. We were also able to plan out worship experiences in advance because the worship team knew where we were going. While this is new to me, planning with the proper away time has been a very helpful process. I gather with the staff every Monday already knowing what I'm going to preach, and our worship director is able to design worship around that sermon. There seems to be greater clarity when we can look at the calendar and know what is coming up on a particular Sunday. Another blessing that came out of this practice was that my devotional time became more focused. Because I know what I am preaching four months out, I use the scripture for the sermon each week as meditation. So all week I am meditating on the scripture I will preach. I believe it helps me preach because the scripture has fed my soul all week long, and on Sunday I am better equipped to feed others what I have been feasting on for seven days.

As I stated I am new at this and there is much more that can be done by getting away from everyone and everything and planning things out. I eventually found others who are much more seasoned at showing their congregations where it is God is leading them. A good friend of mine, Harry White, who pastors Watts Chapel Missionary Baptist Church in Raleigh, North Carolina, has seen fruit in his ministry by painting a clear picture of where they are going. He takes time to prepare sermons and Bible study lessons months ahead. He shares this with the church's minister of music so that music and worship are centered on the word that God has given him. His sermons and Bible studies for the week are all synchronized so that the people of Watts Chapel truly explore a particular text and topic. Each Sunday, printed in the bulletin, are discussion questions for Tuesday and Wednesday Bible study that correspond to what he preaches on Sunday.

Pastor White describes his method of feeding the sheep this way: "First I proclaim it (on Sundays), then I explain it (Tuesdays and Wednesdays)." He's found this to be extremely helpful because he knows what he is preaching and so does the congregation. The Bible studies are more informed and the discussions more fruitful because the congregants know in advance where they are going. Because they know, they look forward to it. This is all possible because Pastor White spends alone time on the mountain with the Lord so that he can lead the people to green pastures.

Idea:

Synchronized sermons and Bible studies so that the entire congregation explores a particular text and topic together. (From Harry White, Watts Chapel Missionary Baptist Church, Raleigh, NC)

Junius Dotson, who pastors St. Mark's United Methodist Church in Wichita, Kansas, saw the need to retreat with the Lord early on in his ministry. He was taught the value of dedicating time for visioning and writing ideas. Pastor Dotson sets aside time in October to plan for the next year with a balance of Old and New Testament scriptures. The sermon topics drive the systems and ministries of the church. Everything, from the curriculum and children's ministry to family ministry, is planned around the sermons six months at a time.

After his alone time with the Lord, Pastor Dotson takes his ideas and sermons to the creative worship team in November. They then plan everything around the preaching calendar and the staff helps to implement it in their particular areas. For example, Pastor Dotson might preach on the subject of service, and the creative worship team would plan a ministry fair that month to coincide with the sermon.

There have been tremendous results from Pastor Dotson carving out, each year, quality time to discern where God is calling him to lead St. Mark's. Some of the fruit that he has seen is that the ministries and ministry leaders seem to be better aligned because everyone is on the same page. They have also seen a reduction in conflict because there is greater clarity and focus because people know where they are going. Pastor Dotson has also noticed higher levels of ministry accountability. When people know where they are going, ministries can actually assess whether or not they meet their objectives. Last, having the pastor lay out his vision six months into the future helps St. Mark's stay focused on and maintain the ultimate objective of making disciples for Jesus Christ.

Idea:

Set aside time each October to plan the next year's sermons. Create a plan balancing Old and New Testament texts, and focus on topics that will drive the ministries of the church, according to the vision you discern from your time with God. Share the plan with the church's ministry leaders, and expect them to plan ministry accordingly, so that all worship and church activities are in sync and aimed in the same direction. (From Junius Dotson, St. Mark's United Methodist Church, Wichita, KS)

Matt Miofsky, pastor of the Gathering in St. Louis, Missouri, takes a few days every six months to discern where God is calling the congregation. Before spending time alone with the Lord, Matt assesses the congregation, via online survey, and meets with his staff to get a sense of the hopes, dreams, and questions the congregation may be wrestling with. This time alone with God and away from the business of the church allows Matt to really discover where the Gathering needs to go as a community of believers.

What Matt brings back to the congregation after his mountaintop time is six months' worth of sermons and sermon series. These sermon topics are based on the needs of the congregation. The sermon themes are first shared with the staff, where he gets feedback so that everything is framed appropriately. The themes are then shared with the media team, worship team, and small-group leaders. That way worship experiences, videos, images, set design, and small-group discussions are all centered on particular sermons.

Pastor Miofsky believes his time away really gives him the opportunity to look at what the congregation needs. He sees that time as the chance to work on the congregation and not just work in the congregation. One of the tangible results that Matt has seen is an increase in the quality of worship because the team has more lead time to prepare. The small groups know where the pastor is going with his preaching because their studies match his sermons. This helps the people better understand the content of the message, and it sticks with them longer. Matt believes this process has helped him become a better preacher.

Idea:

Twice each year, assess the congregation via an online survey tool such as surveymonkey.com. (If congregants are unlikely to participate in an online survey, distribute and collect the survey via post or some other hard copy means.) The survey should elicit the people's hopes, dreams, questions, and issues they are wrestling with. Collect and compile the information. Retreat for a few days to review and pray over it. Allow God to guide you to discover what your congregation needs over the next six-month period. Design your sermons to address those needs. Upon your return, share the plan with your staff, worship teams, small group leaders, and other church leaders, so that they can plan worship and discipleship to coordinate with your sermons. (From Matt Miofsky, The Gathering [United Methodist Church], St. Louis, MO)

Not only does Matt assess the overall direction of the church and the effectiveness of his sermon series, but all of the church leaders do the same. If something doesn't work they find out why and either correct it or avoid doing it again. Matt Miofsky realizes that scheduling a few days away to hear from the Lord is a difficult thing for pastors to do. Many pastors believe they don't have the time and can't afford to do it. However, Matt sticks to his schedule because he believes as the pastor of the Gathering he can't afford not to do it.

Dr. Robert Lee Hill, pastor of Community Christian Church in Kansas City, Missouri, marks off time on his schedule a couple of times a year for sketching sermons, creating special worship services, and planning special events for the church for the upcoming six months or year. Unlike many pastors who take this time to plan ahead, Dr. Hill doesn't tend to physically retreat, although he used to. Now he asks his staff to honor his time—he usually spends at least a day practicing discernment—because "they know I'm working on some 'long-haul' worship-related matters and seeking to get clear about where we as a congregation need to go (as we are led by the Spirit) and what needs to happen in and through my efforts, particularly the preaching, to get us to our intended destination." Dr. Hill says that because he is not a lectionary preacher, this time away to discern the direction God is moving the church is integral to his sermon planning.

Dr. Hill roots his time away in prayer and the reading of scripture. These two practices directly feed the sketching out of his sermons. However, he also takes this quiet time to relax; he reads from some favorite new books, takes a walk, eats a healthy meal, and even sometimes takes a nap.

When his time away is over, Dr. Hill brings back five to seven sermon series, that, with the help and input of his ministerial staff, he will whittle down to three or four. He welcomes suggestions for change from his staff. He also shares the ideas with the worship committee and receives their feedback. The ministerial staff and worship committee vote on the original five to seven ideas by ranking the series in the order of which they would personally prefer and which they believe would most benefit the congregation. They do this planning not blindly but in conjunction with the church calendar, paying attention to special anniversaries in the life of the congregation and forthcoming education programs, justice initiatives, and artistic celebrations so that they can discuss how these events and programs will enhance the new series, and vice versa.

Dr. Hill has experienced the fruit of this time away for himself and for the congregation and staff. It helps the various committees that have to plan their work throughout the life of the congregation. It helps the overall staff because they now know where the church is headed. It helps the preacher because it orients his thinking and spirit as he proceeds with implementing the plan. And lastly, it steers the congregation in a definitive direction, and because of this, they respond with gladness and appreciation. By implementing a plan

---

Idea:

Mark off at least one full day two or three times each year for sermon series planning. Start by reading scripture, then spend time in prayer, review the calendar, read commentaries, read poetry, and read more scripture. Pull out your church's pictorial directory or a list of the members, and pause to think about each person, each family. Spend time in prayer. Take a walk. Eat a healthy meal. Take a nap. Then map out sermons for a six to twelve month period, based on what you feel the Holy Spirit is leading you toward for this congregation. Plan more sermons or series than you will need. After you have a plan on paper, sit with it for a while, ponder and pray over it. As soon as possible take the plan to your program and worship leaders. Together, consider what else is happening in the life of the church during that period of time. Are there important events, church anniversaries, or programs already planned? How might these intersect with the sermons? Take a vote among the leaders, asking them to consider their personal preference and the needs of the congregation. (From Robert Hill, Community Christian Church, Kansas City, MO)

---

to get away from the daily grind of work at the church, Dr. Hill is better able to discern God's will for the congregation, bringing back to his flock a plan for the future that maps out the direction God is leading them.

Tom Berlin serves as the lead pastor of the Floris United Methodist Church in Herndon, Virginia. For years Pastor Berlin has been securing time on his schedule dedicated to hearing from the Lord. For four days each year, he and other pastors get away from the ministry of the church in order to create a preaching calendar and do strategic planning. He spends time praying, thinking, and reading scripture. He also roams the Internet looking at church websites to see what kinds of sermons and sermon series other pastors are offering and talks with the other clergy who get away with him to gather ideas from them. When it is all said and done, the four days result in nine to twelve months of sermon series planning.

What Tom Berlin brings back to the church is a document that gives a brief explanation of the concept of each series. Every sermon is listed with a proposed date, title, and scripture passage; and when there are key verses, those wll be highlighted. Doing this provides the Floris worship team an opportunity to plan music and creative components of worship that tie in to the sermon.

Pastor Berlin reviews the plan with his leadership team and encourages their input. While he reserves the right to do what he believes is in the best interest of the congregation, he allows his team to offer suggestions. This means that sometimes series may be altered, and some series don't make the cut all together. The associate pastor who oversees worship will then take the approved plan to the worship team to design worship around the series. Pastor Berlin is present in those meetings to ensure that what is being designed remains true to the vision for each sermon. This team meets weekly to evaluate the past worship experience as well as to plan the details of the coming week's worship. This process for worship planning is spelled out in Lovett Weems and Tom Berlin's book *Overflow*.[1] Pastor Berlin further elaborated on the effects of the process for me:

> The practice of thoughtful planning enables the pastor to lead Christ's flock from pasture to pasture, where they can be renewed throughout the year, has been helpful for the people of Floris UMC. The volunteers and staff are honored to have the planning done so they can effectively fulfill their ministry assignments. They are able to create visuals, send out communications to the church body and community, post information through social media, and understand how each series will impact everyone from ushers to greeters to sanctuary stewards. Our staff and volunteers are fully supportive of this time and see it as essential to good planning and good relationships.

Tom Berlin explains the benefits of spending quality time alone with the Lord in order to discover where God is calling him to lead God's sheep this way: "It has helped the overall ministry of church because it requires the lead pastor to think through critical issues facing the church; cast vision; and attend to matters like stewardship,

---

Idea:

Each year, schedule four days away with a small group of other pastors to do strategic and sermon planning. Discuss your ideas together, roam the Internet to find additional resources, and collaborate on the task of planning. For sermon series, create a document outlining each series, with dates, titles, and scripture texts. Upon your return, share the proposed plan with your leaders and staff, and allow them to collaborate with you on the ways it will be implemented. Listen to their suggestions and ideas, and incorporate those ideas that will increase the effectiveness of the plan while staying true to your vision for each sermon. This team—including you—should evaluate each week's past worship service. (From Tom Berlin, Floris United Methodist Church, Herndon, VA)

---

service, and discipleship. The series allows communication in the church to have a focus, which enables other ministries to create opportunities connected to the series."

What all of these pastors do during their time with God may be different and what they take back to their congregations may not be exactly the same. But what they all have in common is a strong sense of where they will lead their congregations and how they will get there. These congregations also have a great deal of uniformity in what is being studied as well as clearly defined ministry goals. There is a greater understanding of what's coming next so that people know what to expect. The pastors also share the common belief that in order to feed Jesus's sheep, they must first spend some time with God so that the sheep in their care are fed properly. Jesus often got away from his disciples and away from the crowds so that he could have one-on-one time with the Father. He would then go back to the hustle and bustle of leading people with energy, purpose, and a clear vision of where and how to lead his followers to green pastures. I believe today's shepherds must do the same so that we aren't derailed from our true role. One-on-one time with God is a true way to help pastors identify the mission, the mission field, the vision, and how to share it, so that we as God's shepherds stay on track.

Questions for Reflection

1. Do you believe pastoral mountaintop time could benefit the pastor and congregation? If so, how?

2. What are some things that a congregation can do to ensure that the pastor has an opportunity to spend quality time away with the Lord?

3. What should a pastor do in order to prepare for his or her mountaintop time with the Lord?

4. What are the dangers for the congregation if the pastor never has an opportunity to go the mountaintop?

Notes

Foreword

1. Peter Cartwright, *Autobiography of Peter Cartwright* (1856; repr., Nashville: Abingdon Press, 1984), 267–68. The late Bishop James Thomas first called my attention to this passage.

1. What Is a Pastor?

1. Donald E. Messer, *Contemporary Images of Christian Ministry* (Nashville: Abingdon Press, 1989), 14.

3. Essential: Cast the Vision

1. Howard A. Snyder, *The Divided Flame: Wesleyans and Charismatic Renewal* (Grand Rapids: Francis Asbury Press, 1986), 21.

2. Lovett H. Weems Jr., *Church Leadership*, rev. ed. (Nashville: Abingdon, 2010).

3. Ibid., 39.

4. George Bullard, "The Life Cycle and Stages of Congregational Development," PowerPoint presentation, 2001, accessed December 18, 2013, http://sed-efca.org/wp-content/uploads/2008/08/stages_of_church_life_bullard.pdf.

5. Essential: Develop Leaders around the Vision

1. John Edmund Kaiser, *Winning on Purpose: How to Organize Congregations to Succeed in Their Mission* (Nashville: Abingdon, 2006).

6. Essential: Teach and Preach

1. *Dictionary.com Unabridged*, s.v. "conductor," accessed December 29, 2013, http://dictionary.reference.com/browse/conductor?s=t.

2. Ronald F. Youngblood, *Nelson's New Illustrated Bible Dictionary* (Nashville: Thomas Nelson, 1995), 354.

3. Thomas G. Long, *The Witness of Preaching* (Louisville: Westminster/John Knox Press, 1989), 21.

4. Ibid., 25.

5. James Forbes, *The Holy Spirit and Preaching* (Nashville: Abingdon Press, 1989), 88.

6. *The United Methodist Book of Worship Pastor's Pocket Edition* (Nashville: Abingdon Press, 1994), 32.

7. The Work of the People

1. WCC Commission on Faith and Order, *The Nature and Purpose of the Church: A Stage on the Way to a Common Statement*, Faith and Order Paper No. 181 (Geneva: World Council of Churches, 1998), 41.

2. Ibid.

3. WCC Commission on Faith and Order, Lima, 1982, as cited in Michael Kinnamon and Brian E. Cope, eds., *The Ecumenical Movement: An Anthology of Key Texts and Voices* (Geneva: World Council of Churches, 1997; Grand Rapids: Eerdmans, 1997), 196.

4. Ibid., 191.

5. Harold Lindsell, "Spiritual Gifts: A Biblical Perspective on What They Are and Who Has Them," *Christianity Today* 19 (April 11, 1975): 5.

6. N. T. Wright, "The Letter to the Romans," in *The New Interpreter's Bible: A Commentary in Twelve Volumes*, ed. Leander E. Keck (Nashville: Abingdon Press, 2002), 10:708.

7. Charles E. Hummel, *Fire in the Fireplace: Charismatic Renewal in the Nineties* (Downers Grove, IL: InterVarsity Press, 1993), 61.

8. Mahesh Chavda, *The Hidden Power of the Believer's Touch: The Healing Anointing of Every Believer* (Shippensburg, PA: Destiny Image Publishers, 2001), 42–43, emphasis in the original.

9. Hummel, 76.

10. Carlyle Fielding Stewart III, *Reclaiming What Was Lost: Recovering Spiritual Vitality in the Mainline Church* (Nashville: Abingdon Press, 2003), 43.

11. Hummel, 76.

12. Samuel M. Powell, *A Theology of Christian Spirituality* (Nashville: Abingdon Press, 2005), 130.

13. J. Oswald Sanders, *The Holy Spirit and His Gifts* (Grand Rapids: Zondervan, 1940), 109.

14. Thomas R. Yoder Neufeld, *Ephesians*, Believers Church Bible Commentary, ed. Elmer A. Martens and Willard M. Swartley (Waterloo, IA: Herald Press, 2002), 191, emphasis in the original.

15. Ibid., 186.

16. Francis W. Beare, "The Epistle to the Ephesians," in *The Interpreter's Bible: A Commentary in Twelve Volumes,* ed. Nolan B. Harmon (Nashville: Abingdon Press, 1953), 10:692–93.

17. Neufeld, 184, emphasis in the original.

18. Walter E. Wiest and Elwyn A. Smith, *Ethics in Ministry: A Guide for the Professional* (Minneapolis: Fortress, 1990), 63.

9. Making Change: Pastoral Examples (Time on the Mountain)

1. Lovett H. Weems Jr. and Tom Berlin, *Overflow: Increase Worship Attendance and Bear More Fruit* (Nashville: Abingdon Press, 2013).

CPSIA information can be obtained at www.ICGtesting.com
Printed in the USA
LVOW05s2113130314

377329LV00004B/7/P

9 781426 772535